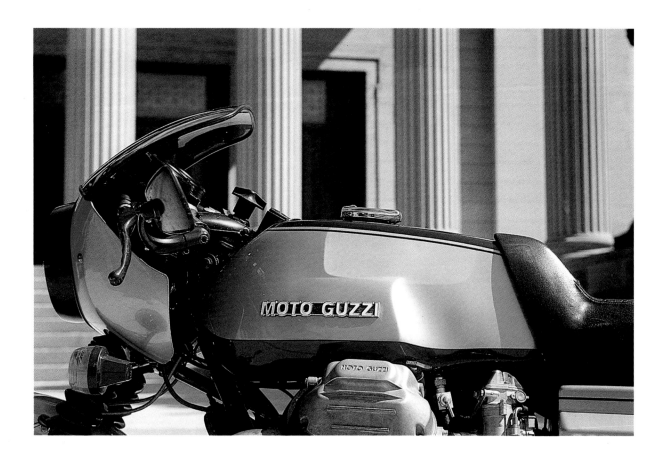

MOTORCYCLE
COLOR·HISTORY

MOTO GUZZI
BIG TWINS

Greg Field
Foreword by Dr. John Wittner

MBI Publishing
Company

First published in 1998 by MBI Publishing Company, 729 Prospect Avenue, PO Box 1, Osceola, WI 54020-0001 USA

MBI Publishing Company books are also available at discounts in bulk quantity for industrial or sales-promotional use. For details write to Special Sales Manager at Motorbooks International Wholesalers & Distributors, 729 Prospect Avenue, Osceola, WI 54020-0001 USA.

Library of Congress Cataloging-in-Publication Data
Field, Greg.
    Moto Guzzi big twins/Greg Field.
        p. cm.—(Motorcycle color history)
    Includes index.
    ISBN 0-7603-0363-0 (pbk.: alk. paper)
    1. Moto Guzzi motorcycle—History. I. Title.
II. Series: motorcycle color history.
TL4486F54   1998
629.227'5—dc21   98-23731

On the front cover: Three generations of Moto Guzzi big twins. The 1995 1100 Sport in the foreground belongs to Rick Engman, and the classic 1973 V7 Sport and the 1967 V700 are owned by photographer Glen Bewley. Glen Bewley

On the frontispiece: Perhaps the most famous Guzzi big-twin model of all time is the 850 Le Mans, this 1978 model is owned by Rob Paetzold.

On the title page: The first series of Daytonas were all monopostos, like this 1993 model owned by John and Mark Mahon. The first fruit of the collaboration between Umberto Todero and Dr. John Wittner, the Daytona demonstrated that there was still life in Mandello del Lario in the 1990s.

On the back cover: A dreamy advertisement (bottom) from Premier Motor Corporation, the U.S. importer of Moto Guzzi motorcycles, connects the two most famous products of the collaboration between Guzzi designers Giulio Carcano and Umberto Todero: the V-8 racer and the V700. After Carcano left Moto Guzzi in 1966, his place was taken by another brilliant designer, Lino Tonti. Tonti's most famous and lasting legacy is the innovative frame he designed for the V7 Sport (top), this one a 1973 model owned by Steve Hamel. A variation of the "Tonti frame" is still in production in 1998.

Edited by Lindsay Brooke
Designed by Rebecca Allen

Printed in Singapore through PH Productions Pte. Ltd.

CONTENTS

FOREWORD

By Dr. John Wittner

The last time I decided to go racing I had no idea where it might lead. I was dreaming of victories and championships, just like anyone who goes racing, but certainly not about working for Moto Guzzi. The idea was just to involve a few of my friends in trying to win a few races with a motorcycle that had been discounted by serious competitors of the time. I knew that I had chosen a good bike, and that I had some very capable friends, but the results of adding those two elements together continues to amaze me even today. Roger Edmondson, then director of the AMA endurance series, said after the first race and win at Rockingham that we had surprised no one more than ourselves. How true that was.

That Moto Guzzi Le Mans III surprised a lot of people too. In retrospect, it was the perfect bike—strong, beautiful, and plenty fast in the hands of riders like Greg Smrz, Nick Phillips, and Noel Portelli. I had always admired the Moto Guzzi twin from my days working in Guzzi dealerships, but I became a real believer in the excellence of its basic design during that first year racing the Le Mans III. The Le Mans 1000 that followed in 1985 was even faster, and we had the best crew chief in the business, Bob Griffiths, to orchestrate the team. That year we won again, against much stiffer competition.

After that we decided to test our mettle sprint racing in Pro Twins competition. It required a new commitment, new strategies, and a new type of motorcycle, which I already had in mind. If I told you all of the things I had to do to keep that pushrod Moto Guzzi engine together spinning at over 10,000 rpm and what incredible riding Doug Brauneck did when the new chassis was not quite on the money, you just wouldn't believe it. There was nothing easy about that year. But over the course of the season, Doug and the bike were the best combination and we won yet another national championship in 1987.

In this book, Greg Smrz says I should have been a NASA engineer, but I don't believe that. I have told Greg on many occasions that he could have been a world champion, and I hope he does believe it. While we obviously have enormous admiration for each other, in truth, the reasons for the stunning success of the team are quite different. Success in racing never depends on the real or imagined brilliance of any one individual. The team brought all of the essential elements together and we managed the available resources according to strategies that we had developed. If there is a hero in the racing story he is a man who few of you know about, Ed Davidson, the team's chief strategist.

From that point on, I was very willingly drawn into the company by Alessandro De Tomaso, a man who loved and supported Moto Guzzi, but remains very much misunderstood by the public. Every year I got in deeper. As the focus on racing wound down over the next few years, my involvement with the Moto Guzzi design team wound upwards. I am very proud of the motorcycles we created working with few financial resources. And I wish that I could tell you about all of the people who were also part of this story, but I am a really poor historian, being more forward-looking by nature. Fortunately, there are good historians and Greg Field is one of the very best.

The amount of work that he has put into this book about the Moto Guzzi big twins must have been staggering. He tirelessly sought out and exhaustively interviewed the most important people in the story. The effort has certainly been worthwhile. You can tell that he has a real feel for the Moto Guzzi story and a love for the bikes. Many rumors have been replaced with fact through his efforts. Even though I lived much of the story and worked with many of those who made the rest of it, I read many things that I had not known. Also, I have to admit my pleasure in reliving my days racing Guzzis

Dr. John Wittner (left) and rider Greg Smrz pose with the 1985 endurance champion racer. *Alan Cathcart*

through the interviews I did and through reading the accounts of those times from Greg Smrz and Doug Brauneck. My highest compliments and thanks go to Greg Field for the fine work that he presents to us.

I am proud and feel lucky to have made some small contribution to Moto Guzzi's history. I hope to continue to do so in the future. I am, likewise, proud that I was asked to contribute to this book. I hope you enjoy reading it as much as I did.

Dr. John

INTRODUCTION AND ACKNOWLEDGMENTS

It seems like nothing dies harder than a moldy old myth. And one of the moldiest in all of motorcycling is that Moto Guzzis are powered by a "tractor" engine first used in the Mechanical Mule, a funky, all-wheel-drive ATV-on-steroids designed for the Italian military. Every book and magazine that mentions Moto Guzzi eventually gets around to retelling it, perhaps because it is the type of faintly disparaging "inside" story that some *giornalista* around the world consider "good copy" nowadays.

So, a word of warning: If you hate stepping outside the comfort zone provided by such myths, skip the first half of chapter 1 or buy another book on the subject. This book is not about a tractor engine. It is about a motorcycle engine, one of the great ones in fact, one that has confounded its critics and delighted Guzzisti for over 30 years.

The real story of how the Moto Guzzi big twin engine came to be is somewhat longer and more complex than the myth, but no less interesting. It involves Italy's oldest motorcycle company and two of Italy's greatest race-bike designers (Giulio Carcano and Umberto Todero) who were pressed into service for a new kind of competition, the results of which would determine the fate of the company. This book is also the story of how Carcano's and Todero's work has been carried forward by other great designers, such as Lino Tonti and Dr. John Wittner, who created such great machines as the Eldorado, V7 Sport, Le Mans, California, Daytona, and many others.

Some may find the organizational structure of the book kind of odd. It is arranged in what I call "chronomodelogical" order. That is, I split the subject into chapters based on what I considered to be compelling characteristics in common. Then within each chapter I group the models by approximate order of introduction and discuss all years of a given model before moving on to the next model, so you can skip right to the section on your bike or the

one you'd like to own. Even so, you may wonder why the Quota models are in chapter 4 with the spine-frame models. They aren't truly spine-frame models, but the Quota frame is close in concept to the spine frame so I stuck them in chapter 4 anyway.

In writing the book, I relied primarily on human sources. This, of course, creates its own risks of inaccuracy because of the vagaries of memory, but these first-person recollections add a dimension to the Guzzi story that couldn't be gotten any other way.

It all started with leads from Dave Richardson of Moto International, so I'd like to thank him first. Dave has written the essential book for owners of Moto Guzzi twins, *Guzziology*, available through his shop or through the Classic Motorbooks catalog. Dave was also incredibly helpful in sharing his unparalleled technical knowledge of the Guzzi twins. Thanks also to Herb and Cam at Moto International for their help.

Next, thanks to Lindsay Brooke for hooking me up with Dr. John Wittner, supplying copies of many magazine reviews, and editing this book.

Dr. John Wittner was kind enough to spend many hours on the phone answering questions about his days racing and giving insight into the design of many of the modern and future Guzzis. He also wrote the foreword for the book. Thanks also to Greg Smrz and Doug Brauneck, who spoke to me of their days riding Dr. John's Guzzis.

Reno Leoni and Mike Baldwin also contributed generously their recollections of campaigning the 850 Le Mans in US Superbike racing. Reno also contributed important details of his time working with Guzzis as a mechanic for the Berliners.

Before long, the trail led to Ivar de Gier. Based on my correspondence with him, I think he knows more of the overall history of Moto Guzzi than any person alive, and he contributed more to the historical sections of this book than any other

The final version of the original 1000 SP was known as the "NT" (for "New Type"). Compared to the first SPs, the NT was given a seat with thicker padding, lower and more forward footpegs, a revised exhaust, less widespread use of flat-black paint, and the option of two red-and-white paint schemes, one as shown on this 1984, and the other the reverse of it.

Famed racer Mike Hailwood tested the red-frame V7 Sport and liked it very much. Unfortunately, though the company tried, it was unable to hire Hailwood to race the Sport. Knowing how great riders such as Hailwood can make all the difference in racing success, it's interesting to speculate how Moto Guzzi's fortunes would have been affected by Hailwood riding the Sport to victory in a prestigious race. *Seth Dorfler collection*

individual. If this were a just world, Ivar would have gotten the contract to write this book, and if we're all really lucky, some publisher will get him going on the complete history of the marque and its motorcycles.

Despite the impediments of distance and language, the following former Moto Guzzi designers, engineers, and executives offered their help: Michele Bianchi, Giulio Carcano, Enrico De Vita, and Lino Tonti.

A key turn of events was in finally tracking down Michael Berliner, former importer of Moto Guzzi into North America. As you'll see, Mr. Berliner was much more than just an importer. He and his brother, Joe, helped shape the fortunes of Moto Guzzi and several other companies by pushing for new models and improvements to compete with the big bikes from Harley-Davidson. Many thanks for all your help. Thanks also to Seth Dorfler and Heinz Kegler, former public-relations man and ace mechanic, respectively, for the Berliners.

Another key to the whole book was the cooperation of Moto Guzzi and the Trident Rowan

Group Incorporated (TRGI). My thanks to the cheerful and thorough help of the following individuals: Eleanora Scali for archive support, Umberto Todero for design insight, Gemma Pedretta for help at a tense moment, Mario Tozzi-Condivi (President of Moto Guzzi) and Howard Chase (Chairman of the Board of TRGI) for discussing the present and future plans of Moto Guzzi, and to Kay Germano for insight into the history of De Tomaso Industries.

No one in America is more associated with Moto Guzzi than is Frank Wedge, director of the Moto Guzzi National Owners Club (MGNOC), which is the friendliest, best run enthusiast's group of all. Everyone who owns a Guzzi should belong to the club. Thanks, Frank, and thanks also to David L. Smith, who runs the European Division of MGNOC, who also helped in many, many ways.

Another guy who seems to know everything about Guzzis is Bob Nolan, the MGNOC rep for Washington state. He and Marian, his wife, have a reputation as being "the nicest people on the planet," and the reputation is well earned.

Very special thanks to another rare pair, Dave and Sharon Hewitt, who were sales representative for Moto Guzzi through the Berliner and most of the Maserati years, for sharing their remembrances, and their archive of sales material and correspondence. I can say with the confidence of hindsight that the biggest mistake, by far, made by any of the American Guzzi importers was when Maserati chose to let the Hewitts go.

Guzzi enthusiast Glenn Bewley made the excellent photo that graces the cover of this book (two of the bikes shown are his). Jon Tree, another camera-wielding Guzzi nut, took the excellent photo of Al Phillips's 850 racer. Special thanks to a third camera-toting Guzzisti, Nolan Woodbury, for helping out on so many shoots, and in so many other ways. Thanks to noted motojournalist Alan Cathcart for use of his photograph of Dr. John and Greg Smrz, and to Dave Edwards of *Cycle World* for allowing me to use two photos from the magazine's archives. Thanks also to Michael Dregni for use of several photographs.

Many former and current dealers and distributors also assisted: Dick Barnes, Dale Bedeaux, Mike and Erolyn Blair, Bob Budschat, Tom Christerson of Sunset Motors, Al Decker of Decker Harley-Davidson, Joe Eish of Eish Enterprises, John and Willy Gregory, Joel Gulbranson, Mike Harper of Harper's Moto Guzzi, Russ Heulitt of Two R's Moto Guzzi, Michael Houdala of Trackstar Cycles, Ken Johnson of Atlas Cycles, Jim Lawton, Bob Lee and Chuck Lee, A.J. Lewis, Bob Raber, Joseph Riso of Ghost Motorcycles, Beno Rodi, Cindy Rutherford of Century Cycle, John Schwartz, Torello Tacchi, Jim Tagaris of Harry's,

Loyal Truesdale, Jonathan White of Domi Racer, and Steve Zabaro.

For allowing me to photograph their bikes, I thank the following individuals: Gary Anderson, Jerry Baranski, Eric Blume, Jim Elms, Michael Gunn, Steve Hamel, John Hansen, Jimmy Huggler, Greg Isley, Brian Jenkins, Kevin Karcher, Terry Kellog, Alan Kolata, Greg Kolle, Rick Mahnke, John and Mark Mahon, Jason Moore, Gary Olson, Rob Paetzold, Al Phillips, Bill Price, Chardon Smith, Kristian Soholm, and Kelly Weiland.

One of the most difficult but enjoyable parts of the research was tracking down the motor officers who rode Guzzis in California. My thanks to the following: Joe Ballister, Howard Barnes, Brett Benson, Ron Brian, Les Clear, Chuck Downing, Scotty Henderson, Mike Lawrence, Wally Maxwell, Herbert C. "Pinky" Meredith, Fred Moeckley, Frank Ortiz, Larry Piatt, Greg Sharp, Joe Schlechter, Gary Smith, Richard C. "Dick" Studdard, Nathan Thibodeaux, John Tutaj, and Gary Williams.

Special thanks to Fabio Andreozzi, Ivar de Gier, Marco Grazziani, Patrick Hayes, Paula Mazzucchi, and Giovanni Sicola for translation services.

Thanks to the following for contributing in myriad ways: Sheldon Aubut, Carrie Carroll and Dan Mullins, Kevin Cruff and Teri Majka, Bob Fariss, Bruce Finlayson, Allan Fritz, Robert Genat, Winston Goodfellow, Jerry Goudie, Mike Parti, Don Ratliff, Scott Rohrer, Clement Salvadori, and all the members of the online Moto Guzzi correspondence list.

For long-term encouragement and support, to my parents, Laurie and Larry; my brothers and sisters Scot, Shawn, Dawn, and Heather; and my good friends Owen Herman, Kevin Lentz, Tim Lien, Tom Samuelsen, John Scharf, and Joe Sova.

For putting me up and putting up with me while in Milwaukee: Annie, Heidi, and Tobie Golembiewski; Ray, Carol, Becky, Katie, Tracy, Vicky, and Nicole Karshna; Ed and Jean Kwiecinski; and Jeff and Jackie Ciardo.

For tolerating my "fluid" deadlines, editor Zack Miller and the rest of the staff MBI Publishing Company.

Finally, to Jeni, who put up with so much obsessive behavior and gave up so much so that I had time to finish this manuscript.

If I have forgotten anyone, I hope they will forgive the oversight.

A final note: Throughout, I use the indefinite pronoun "he" because there's no good substitute acceptable to the bulk of the audience for this book. If use of this term offends you, return your book to the author, care of the publisher, for a cheerful refund on the unread portion.

—Greg Field

CHAPTER 1

THE LOOP-FRAME BIG TWINS:

V700 through Eldorado and 850 GT

As the 1950s gave way to the 1960s, the Italian motorcycle manufacturers were finally confronted with a reality their American counterparts had learned from or succumbed to more than four decades earlier as Ford began to churn out the Model T by the hundreds of thousands: When motorcycles are substantially cheaper than cars, you'll sell a lot of motorcycles to people whose primary interest in them is economical transportation, but when the price equation equalizes or reverses, there are hard times ahead. With the advent of cheap, small cars such as the Volkswagen Beetle, the Morris Mini, and the Fiat 500, Italians began looking on motorcycles more as sporting machines and less as day-to-day transportation. Sales plummeted.

Despite this apparent setback, it was (as the Buddhists are wont to say) an "auspicious time." By the early 1960s, the market for sporting motorcycles in the United States was on an upward ascent that showed no signs of abating. But even in the United States, the market was changing. Where in the 1950s English sporting twins had dominated the market, by the early 1960s the Japanese were taking over the lead. Like the British before them, the Japanese had started small. Before long, however, they too began increasing displacement in an effort to satiate the American demand for ever more horsepower. As fast as the Japanese juggernaut was rolling over the U.S. marketplace, two related motorcycle categories showed a curious lack of competition: heavyweight touring and police bikes. Better yet, this market suffered the same lack of competition in Europe as it did in America.

Why? Maybe because the market was relatively small. Maybe because no other manufacturer had yet worked up the courage to challenge the leaders—Harley-Davidson in the United States, and BMW in Europe—head-to-head, on their own turf.

Into this potentially lucrative void stepped Joe and Mike Berliner, brothers who ran The Berliner Group, one of the most aggressive and successful motorcycle import businesses in the United States, which consisted of the Berliner Motor Corporation (importers of Ducati, Norton, Sachs, and Zundapp motorcycles), the J.B. Matchless Corporation (importers of Matchless motorcycles), and the Premier Motor Corporation (importers of Moto Guzzi motorcycles).

"Our distributors always said, 'We need a big machine, something that is comfortable,' " remembered Mike Berliner. The Berliners were known for listening to the needs of their distributors and dealers, so it came to pass that, long before anyone else had seen the opportunity afforded by this lack of competition, the brothers began looking for someone to build a large, American-style touring and police motorcycle for them.

Let the Contest Begin

But the Berliners weren't the only ones shopping for a new police or touring mount. The 500-cc single-cylinder Moto Guzzi Falcones used by the

Three of Guzzi's great designers: Giulio Carcano (left), Enrico Cantoni (center), and Umberto Todero (right). Carcano and Todero teamed up on several great designs, including the V-8 racer and the V700. *Moto Guzzi*

Second-series Ambassadors were fitted with a new, larger gas tank and Dell'Orto concentric carburetors. They retained the V700-style battery covers and alloy speedo nacelle. Owner Greg Kolle painted and striped the bike and added a few custom touches to his Ambassador, painting the fork and nacelle white.

The fan-cooled engine of the 3x3 Mechanical Mule. This engine was designed by Antonio Micucci and developed by Todero and has little in common with the V700 engine except the 90-degree V-angle. *Moto Guzzi*

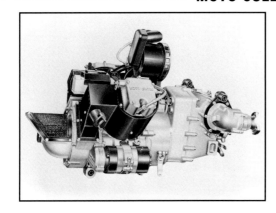

A prototype V700 engine, designed by Carcano and Todero. Compare this engine to Micucci's Mule engine. Though it's made of rough sand castings, all the major pieces are very similar to those on the production engines. Later prototype crankcases were reinforced with three short vertical webs per side, rather than the one rib shown here. After some failures on the first production machines, the case was further reinforced by longer webs. *Moto Guzzi*

Italian police were clearly obsolete for the new Italy that was emerging in the 1960s. Road speeds were higher, cars were ever faster, and at last the Italian Government realized it was time for the police to catch up. The Italian civilian and military police had been riding Guzzis since the 1920s, so Moto Guzzi no doubt expected an exclusive order to develop the new police machine.

Unfortunately, times had changed more than Moto Guzzi realized. Several Italian motorcycle companies (including Ducati) had been taken over by the government, and several others (including Guzzi) were nearing financial collapse. In fact, about all that was keeping Moto Guzzi solvent was the sale of police bikes. Even so, the government couldn't just award a development contract to Moto Guzzi when so many companies were in such desperate need of the business.

The solution for all concerned was an enlightened compromise. In early 1963, the Ministero degli Interni (Ministry of Internal Affairs) turned its search for a new mount into a contest in which everyone involved had a chance of winning in some way. To the government would go its pick of machines custom designed to its specifications, and the government didn't even have to pay design and development costs. To the winning manufacturer

would come the financial security of fat contracts to resupply Italy's police forces. To the losers, the opportunity to adapt their designs for the civilian market. But it was the Italian motorcycle enthusiast who stood to gain the most—a gaggle of new machines to fawn over.

Specifications for the new police/military motorcycle were specific in some respects but were kept deliberately vague in others to allow each manufacturer maximum creativity in designing its contest entry. Requirements included a guaranteed service life of at least 100,000 kilometers without major repairs, easy serviceability without special tools or specialized training, and a high top speed. It also had to have an electrical system designed to handle full police equipment. And it had to be ready for testing in 1966. Faced with ever-declining revenues and the need to spend a lot of money to avoid losing its "cash cow," Moto Guzzi's future hinged on winning this contest—and winning it with a machine that could be mass produced economically enough that the company could quickly recover its development costs.

Enter this chapter's two heroes, Giulio Carcano and Umberto Todero. To Carcano fell primary responsibility for designing Moto Guzzi's entry, and to Todero (long Carcano's right-hand man) fell the task of making the design a reality. Todero had worked for Moto Guzzi since 1939, and Carcano since 1936. Together and with the help of others they had built many of Moto Guzzi's most successful racers (including the awesome *Otto Cilindri*, the 500-cc V-8 racer of the mid-1950s) before being forced into more mundane commercial work following Guzzi's withdrawal from racing in 1957. Even so, their best, most enduring legacy was to come from this, their final collaboration on a motorcycle design.

Starting with a clean slate and the contest specifications, Carcano and Todero quickly got to work in May 1963. They decided that the new machine should have twice the power of the old Falcone, or 45 horsepower. Then, they got out their slide rules and calculated that they could handily get that power with a displacement of 700 cc, so a 700 the new machine would be (actually 703 cc). For simplicity and reduced cost, they decided the new machine would be air-cooled.

Next, the pair set about deciding on engine architecture, since that affected almost every other detail about the motorcycle. In choosing the architecture, they had to balance all the various requirements for the design, from the obvious ones common to designing any engine, to the specific requirements of the contest. Many options were available to them.

Across-the-frame parallel twins, like those on most British machines, allow a reasonably narrow powerplant but less-than-ideal cooling and difficult access to top-end components. Longitudinal V-twins, like those from Harley-Davidson, offer the same advantages and disadvantages as the parallel twins. Flat twins, like those from BMW, offer nearly ideal cooling and good access to top-end components, but at the cost of width and vulnerability of the cylinders and heads to damage.

Given all the requirements of the new machine, one architecture suggested itself—a V-twin with the cylinders splayed across the frame—but the final impetus to select it came from on high. No, not from God, but from a figure held by some to be close to God: Carlo Guzzi, co-founder of the company, and himself a legendary engineer. "Carlo Guzzi proposed the 90-degree V-twin and he encouraged me to realize the project," said Carcano.

The 90-degree angle also gave perfect primary balance, which allowed them to make the engine as vibration-free as possible without the need for balancer shafts. Of equal importance in this case, the architecture allows more of the engine's major components to be accessible without removing the engine from the frame than does any other. Because of its 700-cc nominal displacement and V configuration, the new engine and the bike it would power were designated "V7." (Even so, I'll refer to it as the "V700" to avoid any possible confusion with the later V7 Sport.)

Carcano and Todero weren't the first motorcycle engineers to design a 90-degree transverse (cylinders transverse, crankshaft longitudinal) V-twin motorcycle engine. Legendary British designer George Brough had used the across-the-frame architecture for both a twin and a four in the 1920s and 1930s. American, German, Italian, and Japanese designers

also gave the transverse 90-degree V-twin a try, but because of shortcomings, these designs never caught on.

Individually, Carcano and Todero had each worked on 90-degree Vs in the past. Carcano had designed an air-cooled 600-cc engine designed to power the Fiat 500 car, and Todero had helped develop the fan-cooled 750-cc engine for the 3x3 Mechanical Mule, an engine designed by another Moto Guzzi engineer, Antonio Micucci.

Neither the Fiat 500 nor the Mule engine was used as the basis for the V700 engine, however, and it's somewhat puzzling how the whole misconception got started, given the fact that the Mule engine was designed by Micucci, rather than by Carcano. The fact is, all the V700 engine and the other two share in common is a 90-degree V-angle. "Comparing the head design and structure, the distribution, displacement, lube and fuel systems, and engine crankcases is enough to demonstrate that the engines are totally different and come from different ideas," asserted Todero. Said Carcano on the issue: "The [Mule] engine has nothing in common with the V7. It had a forced cooling system and was a 90-degree V, but its cylinders, heads, and engine casing, etc., differed completely." Further supporting their claim is an argument put forth by Michele Bianchi, who came to Moto Guzzi in 1964 as the company's export manager: If Carcano and Todero were merely copying the Mule engine, why would they not make the new engine in the Mule's "classical" displacement of 750 cc, rather than the "anomalous" displacement of 703 cc?

It's interesting to note that the other companies participating in the contest—Benelli, Ducati,

A photograph of the very early civilian prototype V700. Early prototypes had the rearward-pointing gas-cap lever (a lawsuit waiting to happen), no battery covers, single seat, hooded headlight ring, rectangular taillight, and only one reinforcing rib on each side of the crankcase.
Cycle World

Berliner sales reps Dave and Sharon Hewitt had this V700 prototype in the spring of 1966 to show to their dealers. Hewitt put about 2,000 miles on the prototype over the two months he showed it all over his territory before passing it off to Jim Tagaris of Denver, Colorado. When Tagaris was done with it, West Coast distributor Bob Blair picked it up and took it to California.

Gilera, and Laverda—though faced with the same design specifications as Moto Guzzi, all settled upon a common architecture, the vertical twin, with chain final drive and smaller displacement than Guzzi's. That Carcano and Todero had chosen more wisely than the other designers soon became apparent when the machines were put to the test.

With displacement and architecture decided, Todero started sketching. By the end of May, he had completed a drawing of the machine in 1:5 scale. According to Ivar de Gier, who was shown the drawing by Todero, the sketch looks very much like the later V700 prototype. The main difference between the initial drawing and the prototypes later tested was the frame. At first, Todero sketched a frame built from all straight tubes. "Later studies would prove this frame to be too expensive in production, so it was dropped in favor of a cradle frame like seen on the later V7," according to de Gier. Design work on the individual components of the new motorcycle continued through the rest of 1963 and early 1964.

In early 1964, Carcano and Todero began building the first prototype of the new design. Though Carlo Guzzi had been forced to the company sidelines by advancing illness (sadly, he suffered from Alzheimer's disease), he kept an eye on

the developing design until his death in November of that year, about the time the first V700 prototype was completed. The old era at Moto Guzzi had ended and the first manifestation of the new was about to take to the road.

With only a year to go before complete machines had to be submitted for government testing, Carcano, Todero, and several Guzzi test riders began wringing out the new design to be certain it would be ready in every way. The machine proved promising enough that Moto Guzzi began looking beyond potential police sales.

Back in the USA

The Berliners began their search for a new police and touring machine in Bologna. Because of their success at selling Ducati motorcycles in the United States, the Berliners wielded great influence at the factory. They also saw Ducati as the most likely company in their sphere to successfully design and build their new machine. Joe Berliner approached the company in 1962 with an offer to fund the development of an all-new machine for the American market. Soon after, the Berliners took the next logical step, according to Mike Berliner: "What was selling at that time in the United States: Harley-Davidson! So in order to really show them what we wanted, we sent two Harley-Davidsons to Italy—one to Ducati, and one to Moto Guzzi." (Note: None of the Moto Guzzi personnel interviewed for this book recalls ever getting a Harley during this era, but Michele Bianchi recalls getting one from Berliner in 1969 to give to a friend of his in Italy.)

By late 1963, Ducati's Fabio Taglioni had designed and built his vision of what Joe Berliner had ordered: the air-cooled, 1,260-cc V-4 Ducati-Berliner Apollo—the original Ducati "Monster." The engine Taglioni designed was distinctly Italian—in fact, what would later come to be thought of as distinctly Ducati. Basic architecture of the engine is a double of what would later gain fame as the Ducati L-twin that in much-updated form is still being built today.

Other than the engine, the whole Apollo package was clearly influenced by the Harley-Davidson, as one look at the photo of it will probably convince you. Dave Hewitt, an independent sales representative for the Berliner Group who helped uncrate the machine when it got to the United States,

summed up its looks: "It was ugly, but it wasn't ugly enough to be cute."

It was also a powerful and intimidating machine. After uncrating the monster, they looked it over thoroughly, and that's when Berliner began having doubts about the machine his brother had commissioned. "The only problem I saw with the machine was the chain," Berliner remembered. "When you have a four-cylinder with power like it had, you better have a chain that can pull the *Titanic*." They put it on its centerstand, filled it with gas, and fired it up. At first it wasn't running right, hitting only on a couple of cylinders "sitting there going blat, blat, *splat*," according to Hewitt. It was also in gear—whether that was on purpose or by mistake, none of the principals seems to remember. With each *splat*, the tire would expand in size from the sudden increase in centrifugal force. "I was afraid to get on the Apollo—I don't mind telling you," Berliner continued. "I went on every machine but the Apollo. When I had it on the stand and opened the throttle and saw that the tire started

DUCATI/Berliner - APOLLO 1260 cc.

Joe Berliner commissioned Ducati to design and build this interesting machine, the Ducati-Berliner Apollo. Powered by a 1,260-cc V-4 engine, the Apollo was meant to compete for police and touring customers with the Harley-Davidson big twins. According to the Berliner spec sheet, two versions were to be offered, the 100-horsepower four-carb version (shown) and the 80-horsepower two-carb version. Only one prototype and one spare engine were built. Note the square-section front downtube, ram-air scoops under the tank, distributors (one on each side), and overall Harley mimicry. The Japanese didn't fire the first shot in that war; Ducati did. Because of its cost and complexity, the Apollo was not put into production. Fortunately, the Berliners soon had the V700 Moto Guzzi with which to take on Harley-Davidson. *Seth Dorfler collection*

The more finished civilian prototype, painted silver, with black striping. By this time, three webs were cast in below the cylinder on each side of the crankcase. The actual production machine would look very similar to this prototype. Changes included the "sissy bar" behind the seat replaced by individual grab rails along each side of the seat, a reshaped seat with a removable strap, and a reversed gas-tank lever (so it pointed forward). The small hood portion of the headlight ring was deleted, and the gas tank, battery covers, and toolboxes were painted red. Note the tiny opening on the rear of the muffler. These mufflers were used on world-version V700s. American-market machines got revised mufflers, with larger openings. *Cycle World*

swelling up, I said, 'Forget it! I won't get on that thing.'" As they continued fiddling with the throttle, it suddenly kicked in with all four cylinders, and remembered Hewitt, "we had a minor explosion because it spun the tire on the rim and tore the stem out of the inner tube."

After he had it road-tested, Berliner was convinced the Apollo would accomplish its mission: "It would have completely challenged Harley-Davidson. Nobody could have touched it, with the four cylinders and all that unbelievable horsepower." It was a stable, comfortable highway machine, too, according to Heinz Kegler, a mechanic for Berliner, who tested the bike. "It felt heavy and stable, like a big Buick," Kegler said. Berliner believed so strongly in it that he had sales literature printed up, listing two versions that would be offered.

Unfortunately, the Apollo was also complex and expensive to manufacture, so the Italian government officials who oversaw Ducati decided the company would not proceed with production of the machine, according to Berliner. Fortunately, there was a Plan B.

About the same time as the Apollo production deal fell through, Joe Berliner first set eyes on an interesting new project from his other Italian affiliate. On a visit to the Moto Guzzi factory, Berliner was shown a prototype of the new V700 and realized immediately the possibilities. Before him was a motorcycle that struck an almost perfect balance between the too-massive Harley and the reliable but anemic BMW. To Berliner, it must have seemed that the Guzzi engineers had read his mind. He is reputed to have exclaimed, "Build it for us. *Now!*" While Moto Guzzi had no doubt been considering

the possibilities of a civilian version of its new military/police prototype, this was just the push the nearly bankrupt company needed to make the civilian V700 a reality.

Prototype Testing

Testing continued through most of 1965, during which changes were made, including experimentation with several different carburetor sizes, including 34-, 32-, 30-, and 29 millimeters. In the end, 29-millimeter Dell'Orto SSI carbs were chosen and carried over onto the production machines. These test hacks definitely resembled the final production V700, having similar looking frame, engine, transmission, rear drive housing, toolboxes, exhaust pipes, mufflers, fork, headlight bucket, and instrument nacelle to those used on the production machines. Other parts differed markedly from those on the first production machines, including the front fenders and its stays, the gas tank (from the utility version of the Falcone) with the rearward-pointing gas-cap hold-down lever, the rectangular taillight, and the "hooded" headlamp ring. Photos of these early prototypes show them fitted with solo saddles and lacking battery covers. Judging from the photos, finish appears to be gray on the tank and black on the frame, fenders, fork, headlight bucket, and toolboxes.

Word began leaking out about the new machine as the prototypes became a common sight on the roads around Mandello. The earliest mention of the V700 that I found in the U.S. press was in a brief article in the May 1965 *Cycle World*, which shows photos of a prototype civilian V700. Specifications listed in the article generally match those of the later production machines except that the power is listed at 42 horsepower (eight less than later machines) and it has a single-disc clutch (rather than twin-plate).

By November 1965, the civilian prototype had been considerably refined, looking much more like the final production configuration than the earlier prototypes had. New parts included a bench seat, battery covers, a chrome-plated passenger hand rail that also forms a short sissy bar behind the seat, and decals for the gas tank and battery covers (see the photos). It was in this form that the civilian V700 made its public debut, at the Milan exposition that month.

The V700 didn't reappear in a U.S. magazine until the February 1966 *Cycle World*, in an article by Carlo Perelli on the 1965 Milan show. No photo was shown of the V7, but Guzzi's new big twin was briefly mentioned in the text, along with its basic specs, which included a projected top speed of 140 miles per hour (!) and a price in Italy of $1,040.

Let the Testing Begin

By early 1966, prototype testing had proved that Carcano and Todero had succeeded brilliantly, and their preproduction V700 was ready for the government tests. Before the tests began, Ducati dropped out because it was unable to get its entry finished in time.

According to Ivar de Gier, the first stage of testing was to compare the Italian twins with the "worldwide 'standard' police bike, the BMW R69S." After this comparison, the test-riding phase began. One of the goals of this testing was to see which, if any, of them were able to meet the specification for 100,000 kilometers of riding before major maintenance was necessary. The Guzzi proved so superior that the government testers decided that there was no point in completing this phase of testing. After only 31,000 kilometers had been ridden, the Guzzi was unanimously chosen the winner of the riding phase of the test. Even so, Moto Guzzi resolved to finish the 100,000 kilometers with its own test riders at the controls to see how its machine would do. Unfortunately, they got bored, too. "Guzzi's own test riders rode another 55,000 kilometers on it," according to de Gier, "so with a total of 86,000 kilometers, the bike was dismantled for inspection. The result was good. Piston and cylinder changing was not necessary, crankshaft bearings were like new, as was the big end and the gearbox. Only the cosmetics were a bit poor."

The next phase of testing was to compare the machines for ease and cost of maintenance. As good as Guzzi had done in the other phases, this one was a slam-dunk for the new V-twin. Compared to the chain-drive parallel twins submitted by the other contestants, the Guzzi was a mechanic's dream. When the final scores were tallied, the clear winner was the twin that Carcano and Todero had

A photo from the July 1966 *Cycle World*. Way in the background, behind the Guzzi V-8 racer is a black-painted V700 prototype that was displayed at the *Cycle World* show in Los Angeles in spring of 1966. No one seems to remember whether this was the same machine Dave Hewitt had, and was repainted black, or whether it was a second prototype sent to the United States. Little-known side note: Honda paid Moto Guzzi quite a bit of money in the early 1970s to borrow the V-8 and study it closely. *Cycle World*

designed from day one to be the perfect police bike. Moto Guzzi soon would receive contracts to outfit the Polizia Stradale (highway police), Polizia Urbana (city police), Caribinieri (military police), and the Corazzieri (the presidential guard). Production was to commence late in 1966.

By winning the contest, Carcano and Todero likely saved the company, which had been put into receivership on February 25, 1966. While the Italian government is known for the extreme lengths to which it will go to keep ailing industries from failing, even it has limits to how much they will subsidize a company. Without the promise of revenue from the new police bikes, Moto Guzzi may never have been able to get the funds to implement the real solution to its financial problems: mass production of the civilian version of the V700.

Unfortunately, Carcano would not be around to improve on his new machine. In November 1966, the government agency IMI (Instituto Mobiliaire Italiano) took control of the company, and fired everyone, forcing each to come in and ask for his job back. After 30 years of excellent design work for Moto Guzzi, Carcano felt (rightfully) that it was beneath his dignity to beg government bureaucrats for a job, so he walked away from the motorcycle industry forever. Carcano is still bitter about the shameful mistreatment, but he is also still loyal to Moto Guzzi, and seldom speaks of the affair. When asked by the author about it, he would only say, "The new directors of Moto Guzzi released me." After leaving Moto Guzzi, he never again designed motorcycles, turning his talents instead to his true passion, racing boats, some of which have won world championships.

In February 1967, a new company was formed to control Moto Guzzi, SEIMM (Societa Esercizio Industrie Moto Meccaniche). And in June a worthy successor was hired to carry on where Carcano had left off: Lino Tonti. At the same time, managing director Romolo De Stefani hired another important character in the Moto Guzzi saga, a dynamic racer, tuner, and test rider named Luciano Gazzola, who De Stefani hoped would be the perfect partner for Tonti in developing the next Guzzi motorcycles.

A very early production or pre-production V700 for the U.S. market. Note the changes to the mufflers, headlight ring, gas-cap lever, paintwork, seat, grab rails, and taillight. This machine has white pinstriping around the tank panels and blue "V7" decals on the battery covers. Most production machines had black striping and white "V7" decals (with a black outline) and "700 cc" in black, below the "V7." *Dave and Sharon Hewitt collection*

V700 Prototype in America: "That Oughta Put Harley in Its Grave"

While the Italian government tests were still in session, the Berliners began introducing the new Moto Guzzi grand tourer to the American public. "I remember we were in Daytona, 1966," said Reno Leoni (formerly "Rino," who changed his name to avoid having it mispronounced as "Rhino" by Americans, and who was a mechanic for Berliner at the time), "and the prototype was there when we got back." That comment suggests an arrival date of March 1966 for the prototype V700. It was first displayed at a dealer meeting in New Jersey and was then loaned out to several of the Berliner distributors to show to the dealers who couldn't attend the meeting in New Jersey. It was basically like the civilian prototypes shown at Milan, but it was painted red and silver, similar to the eventual production machines.

Dave Hewitt, independent sales representative, was the first to lay hands on the prototype and got it in time to take it up to Des Moines, Iowa, for the Clymer motorcycle exposition in the spring of 1966. According to Hewitt it was kind of crude and in several respects had many "fiddled-at-the-

factory" parts on it that were different than those of the production machines: "The fenders and battery covers were hand-hammered, and everything was sand cast and was extremely rough and square edged." Hewitt took it upon himself to ride the prototype:

I put around 2,000 miles on it. It was really, really smooth. When you put it in third gear, it just seemed like it was gonna wind and wind forever. It wasn't necessarily going that fast, but it was like being on the end of a long bungie cord. It just pulled forever—and smoothly.

Notwithstanding a few criticisms, the dealers liked the new machine, and Hewitt heard one dealer predict, "That oughta put Harley in its grave."

You might ask how he knew its fenders were hand-hammered:

I ran over a beer can on the Dallas-Fort Worth Freeway—and that's when beer cans were steel. It clamped around the tire and ran up between the fender and the tire and I did a front-wheel stop from 65 miles per hour on the only V7 in America. Luckily, I didn't go down, but it put a flat spot on the tire from sliding all the way to a stop. When I went to repair the fender, I found out that it was made of four or five strips of steel bent and brazed together, with great gobs of Italian body putty to finish it. So it was doubly hard to repair.

The Quick-Release Castration Lever

Hewitt kept the prototype for six weeks or so, and wrote a report, summing up the comments of the dealers and his own observations. One thing he noted with great alarm was that the pointy end of the quick-release lever for the gas cap pointed rearward, right at the rider's crotch, just as it had on the earlier Guzzis. It wasn't just a *potential* for mayhem that he saw in that poorly planned piece—he had experienced it firsthand:

> One time on a Guzzi ISDT, which had the same setup, I put the wheel in a hole and went over the handlebars and it ripped the crotch out of my pants. I took a picture of me standing there with the crotch hanging down on my pants, and that's how we got them to turn it around so it pointed to the front.

Other comments in his report addressed the fact that he had to patch three flaws in the transmission case that were leaking, that there were still some flaws in the crankcase near the oil pan, and that the method of using the centerstand was too confusing.

We Want It *Louder:* The U.S. Mufflers

To a man, every dealer interviewed by the author who was shown the prototype had the same comment about the mufflers, expressed by long-time Guzzi dealer Ken Johnson of Atlas Cycles: "Everybody said 'Look how small that hole is; you can barely stick your finger in it.'" The mufflers on the U.S. prototype were like those later fitted to the V7s built for every market but the United States. It wasn't just a larger opening the dealers wanted; they also asked for a throatier sound. When factory representatives were informed of these requested changes, "They said the horsepower would drop if they did that," continued Johnson. "We said we didn't care. We wanted it open and *louder.*" The report Hewitt wrote on the prototype suggested that a muffler redesign wasn't necessary; all they had to do was "cut off the end of the muffler." On the production machines, U.S. dealers got louder mufflers with bigger openings, and (not surprisingly) power increased slightly.

Cycle World Exposition, 1966

Meanwhile, Carcano's and Todero's two most important designs—the V700 and the *Otto Cilindri,* the water-cooled V-8 500-cc racer—were brought together several thousand miles from home, in Los Angeles, California, for the annual *Cycle World* exposition. Both are shown on the cover of the July 1966 *Cycle World,* the V-8 out front and the V700 in the background. The interesting thing about *this* V700, other than that it was in the United States long before the regular production machines, is that it is painted black with a white pinstripe around the tank panel and a white "V7"

The first American ad for the new Guzzi V700 ran in the March 1967 issue of *American Motorcyclist.*

decal on the battery cover. It also has the wrap-around sissy bar instead of individual passenger grab rails. A stock, black Guzzi V-twin would not be seen in the States again for almost three years.

The first U.S. magazine test of the V700 was in the August 1966 *Cycle World.* Italian motojournalist Carlo Perelli devoted his entire "Report From Italy" monthly column to the new Guzzi. The bike shown in the accompanying photos must have been a late prototype, painted silver or gray with a white stripe around the tank panel. Though there are no real revelations in the article, it does say that production was to begin in the fall. Perelli was enthusiastic about the machine, concluding that it was "a big, good beast, powerful, yet tractable, really built to last a lifetime." The V700 is mentioned again in that issue by publisher Joe Parkhurst in his "Round Up" column. Parkhurst had visited the Moto Guzzi factory and talks about the "650-cc V-7" that was to be available later that year.

A police replica 1970 V700. Police versions of the V700 were officially offered through about 1976, but were available on special order as late as 1978. Later V700s were given the updated parts (such as the larger gas tank, "waffle" crankcases, and dual instruments) used on the V7 Special/Ambassador and the 850 GT/Eldorado.

Readying for Production

With the contest won, the struggle began to turn the hand-built prototypes into production machines. Letters supplied by Dave Hewitt show that by late February 1967, V700s had already reached dealer showrooms in the United States, had had problems, and fixes were on the way. Given that the Italian police departments got the first machines, that it takes time to ramp up production so that a large batch of machines can be shipped to an export market, and that those machines were probably in ports, customs, and the hold of a ship for several weeks, it seems unlikely that they could have been produced in early 1967, so production probably began no later than December 1966.

The first 50 machines went to the Italian Corazzieri in very early 1967. These first Corazzieri machines are unique in that they have more deeply valanced front fenders, special crashbars that sweep back along the header pipes, special leg shields, special badges on the front fender, and special hard saddlebags. They were painted black.

Civilian Production V700s

The civilian V700s were painted like the American prototype had been: Black frame, red gas tank with chrome side panels, and silver-gray fenders, battery covers, and toolboxes. This would remain the standard civilian color scheme until late 1968. Undoubtedly, however, if an importer wanted a special color, the factory supplied it.

Moto Guzzi had high hopes for the new machine in a worldwide civilian market that included 60 countries. Major markets were projected to be Italy, Germany, and the United States, especially if the major police forces could also be convinced of the new Italian heavyweight's merits.

The V700 in America

When the first production V700s arrived in the United States, the workers at Premier Motor Corporation found that Moto Guzzi had lived up to the standards set on shipments of the earlier small Guzzis Premier had been selling since the early 1960s: Each was shipped fully assembled, with the proper fluids in the engine, transmission, and rear drive. Once out of the crate, all the dealer had to do to make it showroom-ready was attach the handlebars, adjust the cables, fill the dry-charged battery, and put gas in the tank. While this undoubtedly contributed to the somewhat high retail price of $1,439 (FOB New York), the difference was likely made up in that the dealer wouldn't have to add a setup charge for the many hours necessary to prepare a partially assembled machine, as was the rule at the time. Even at this price, however, the Guzzi was almost $400 cheaper than the Harley FLH and about the same as the BMW R69S.

Crates soon began moving out of Premier's New Jersey headquarters to dealers around the United States, who uncrated their shiny new machines and eagerly awaited the throngs of new customers they hoped would soon show up. Problem was, the first advertisement had yet to appear in the national magazines. The first one the author was able to find was in the March 1967 *American Motorcyclist*. It may have been slightly late, but at least it was well placed, on the inside of the front cover.

In general, sales came slowly at first, but that depended on the vagaries of the local market. The Midwest, for example, had always been a strong market for touring bikes, whereas California was a sport bike market. "The market niche they were after was the Harley-Davidson—the big luxury tourer," explained Steve Zabaro, parts manager for ZDS Motors in Glendale, California. "But in our area, it was a sport market because every stretch of desert was a potential playground."

Some of the first machines passed through the hands of distributor John Gregory in Kenosha, Wisconsin, and out to his dealer network, including Al Decker of Decker Harley-Davidson in Madison. Many Midwestern dealers, like Decker, had no trouble selling their first V700s. Decker got three of the very early machines. He quickly sold two and decided to keep one for himself. Torello Tacchi, who ran a dealership with his father in Chicago, Illinois, had similar success: "It wasn't a tough sell. You could look at that thing, and it was so massive and so brawny that it just looked like a real macho bike—except for the damn paint job." Like many other dealers, Tacchi thought that red and silver were the wrong colors.

The colors weren't an impediment for other dealers, including those in Dave Hewitt's territory: "They sold pretty easily. When the guys who had been on BSAs and Triumphs got to where they wanted a touring bike, they really had the choice of Guzzi or BMW. And many of them had been insulted by BMW riders and wouldn't own them, so they bought Guzzis."

It Takes a Real Animal to Sell the Goose

Unfortunately, Kenosha dealer and distributor John Gregory had his V700s sit on the floor for quite a while. The local riders mostly gravitated toward sport machines and the Guzzi didn't quite fit the mold. "I couldn't sell 'em," remembered Gregory, "because everyone thought they were big and ugly." Even so, Gregory was confident that given the chance, the Guzzi would prove to be a good seller, but he just needed a good opportunity to show what the V700 was made of.

That opportunity came in the person of Don "Whitey" Ratliff, renowned local hell-raiser. "Whitey was a real animal, a wild man," continued Gregory. "He used to routinely blow up Sportsters, doing burn-outs all over town." When Whitey came in looking for his next motorized victim, Gregory steered him toward the Guzzi. Whitey went home with one because "I thought it looked kinda tough," he remembered, and the first thing he did was lightly chop it by cutting back the fenders and adding a custom seat and small rear light. "It looked pretty nice, really," said Gregory.

True to his reputation, the second thing he did was see if he could blow it up. "One time, he rode into the bar, put the front wheel against the pool table, dropped it into gear, held it wide open, and burned a hole right through the flooring, into the concrete below," remembered Gregory. "The bartender was hollering and yelling at him, but Whitey just kept doing it, with a big grin on his face. Whitey always liked to piss people off. It was quite a spectacle."

And Whitey's efforts soon began to make a difference: "People figured that if Whitey couldn't

Frank Latchin of the Chicago Bureau of CBS News used this V700 to carry newsreel footage between stations in the Chicago area. Note the bar-end turn signals, right-side siren, and police lights. *Dave and Sharon Hewitt collection*

Yes, that's "Tricky
Dick" Nixon in
the back of that
limousine, escorted
by Corazzieri V700s.
Moto Guzzi

make it blow, no one could," according to Gregory. "When people saw what a tough bike it was, they started buying them." And Whitey's Guzzi was around for a while to keep impressing the locals. "I never could blow it up, remembered Whitey. "When I traded it in, it had 80,000 miles."

The First Road Test

A few ads notwithstanding, the V700 got its first real U.S. exposure in the June 1967 *Cycle*, which gave it a very positive review. *Cycle* nicknamed it the "persuader," and the testers were very complimentary about its braking, handling, and comfort. They were even pleasantly surprised at its performance, commenting that "it sprinted . . . sort of like those 230-pound pro-football tackles who can do a hundred yards in ten seconds flat."

Problems and Solutions

Like many first-year designs, the 1967 V700 had a few rough edges and minor design shortcomings. But considering that the V700 was also the first civilian big twin Moto Guzzi had ever built, it was astonishingly trouble-free. The following changes are recorded in parts books or in other documents. Since most of these changes were listed by the engine or frame number, it is seldom clear whether they occurred in 1967 or a later year.

Cracking Cases

A rare, major problem showed up very early in the production run. The first machines had crankcases similar to the cases on the prototypes, with the three short reinforcement webs on the sides of the case below the cylinders. Apparently, these were prone to cracking from the rear cam bearing down to the boss for the rear main bearing, according to Reno Leoni. He also remembers two Guzzi technicians coming to New Jersey for several months to make modifications to the new machines, swapping out crankcases on some (he remembers a whole shipping container of them being shipped back) and the camshafts and related bits on others (this is discussed later in this section).

Former Guzzi dealer Al Decker had three such machines. Soon after getting the machines, he was notified that engines were being recalled, and Premier shipped to him engine short blocks (all but the cylinder heads) to swap into those machines. While the following letter from the archive of Dave Hewitt doesn't actually mention the engine cases, it likely addresses the recall mentioned by Decker. The letter, dated February 24, 1967, was sent to the dealers by Premier:

> 72 of the initial shipment of Moto Guzzi V700s had the wrong specifications. What this means, I do not know. Mike stated that Dr. Bianchi [Moto Guzzi's export manager] phoned him and requested that these 72 units be returned. The exact reason has something to do with internal parts. American units evidently have larger rods, gears, or something. We don't know the extent of the American modifications, but evidently, it is considerable for the abuse we give equipment. The V700s are produced for Egypt, England, and in all 60 countries. The dealers receiving these machines are being notified.

Although Hewitt doesn't remember having any machines in his territory recalled, he said, "I always wondered if that was just a cover for bad crankcases. You can't tell me they don't turn them the same rpm in Egypt as they do here."

Most production machines were fitted with a revised crankcase with larger and more numerous reinforcement webs.

Noisy Valvetrain

Excessive mechanical noise also plagued the early V700s. The first source of noise to be addressed was from the cam and valvegear. As Heinz Kegler said, "It wasn't a mechanical problem, just noise. No matter what you did to the valve clearance, it was still noisy." While the first of the breed may have been noisier than those that came later, part of the problem no doubt was that the cylinder heads jutted up close to the rider's ears. Nevertheless, Moto Guzzi recognized that there was a problem and did its best, short of fitting hydraulic lifters, to fix it.

As soon as the parts were ready, they began fitting each new machine with a revised camshaft, pushrods, and rocker-arm adjustment screws. The camshaft had redesigned ramps and the radii on the ball head of the adjustment screw and the mating socket on the top cap of the pushrods were changed for quieter action.

The new parts were probably first fitted shortly before May 24, 1967, when the problem and new parts were first mentioned in a service bulletin. According to Reno Leoni, two technicians from Moto Guzzi stayed in New Jersey for about two months retrofitting these parts on new machines in the warehouse. These parts were also retrofitted to the noisiest of the machines already sold, by Berliner personnel or by the dealers. The retrofit was of questionable effectiveness. Some dealers who had experience with Panhead Harleys even resorted to the old trick of gluing a thick piece of felt to the inside of the rocker cover. According to Dave Hewitt, the only real solution was to "wear a full-face helmet."

But it may not have been the valvetrain after all, but rather the oil, according to Torello Tacchi, who was a dealer and who helped run the service school in 1969:

Up until 1969, we were instructing the dealers to run 50-weight oil in the summer, and 30-weight in the winter. Well, at the service school with the Guzzi engineers, the question came up, "Why is the engine so noisy until it heats up?" The Italians looked at each other kind of puzzled. I said to them in Italian, "Look, I have one myself, and it's noisy when it's cold. But as soon as it warms up, the noise goes away." And the first thing the guy says is, "What kind of oil do you use?" I told him we were told by Berliner to run 50-weight in the summer and 40- or 30-weight in the winter. Man, he went berserk! He said, "No! No! You have to use multigrade oil!" And by God, we looked in the instruction manual and it specified multi-grade. Lo and behold, when I changed to multi-grade oil on my V7, that sucker started right up and was quiet!

Helical Gears

Straight-cut gears for first through fourth were fitted to early V700s. Like all straight-cut gears, they were noisy, so the factory began fitting a revised gearset that substituted helical gears for second through fourth gears. Apparently, though,

some of the straight-cut gearboxes were especially noisy. Dave Hewitt joked that "On some of them, you'd be riding your motorcycle down the road, and the car in front of you would pull over off the road like you had a siren on." The date this change was made isn't known, but a clue can be drawn from a letter dated March 21, 1968, from Mike Berliner to Jack Gregg:

In reference to our telephone conversation, the only way you can determine if the V7s have helical gears in the transmission is by noting the case number in which the V7 was delivered. The helical gears start with case number 111/156. Anything above this number has the latest equipment. This number can be found on the invoice sent to the dealer.

I fully agree that this is stupid and we should be in a position to tell you from what engine number the above changes have been made. However, we have complained to the factory, and they have promised that in the very near future they will change the method of identification to numerical sequence.

Later, the factory sorted out the numbers because the parts book lists that all the gears used up to number 2119 are different from those used later. This change may refer to the change to helical gears or it may refer to a change in ratios for first and second gear that is hinted at in the workshop manual. The V700 rider's handbook and parts of the workshop manual refer to the gearing of 1.933:1 for first and 1.263:1 for second, which was apparently used on the early V700s. Other parts of the workshop manual refer to new first and second ratios of 2.230:1 and 1.333:1, the same

Late in 1968, a revised version of the V700 was introduced in Europe. Changes include a white paint scheme with revised pinstriping, a rectangular taillight like the one used on the V700 prototypes, and a reshaped seat. Some of these were brought to the United States, but with the regular round taillight. *Moto Guzzi*

lower (higher numerically) ratios later used on the Ambassador. This change to the gearing may have been made at the same time as the change to helical gears or it may have been made at another time.

Transmission Leaks and Throw-Out Bearings

Unfortunately, the Guzzi four-speed also gained a reputation for leaking. The main culprit was the breather, which was nothing more than a hole in the bolt on the left side of the transmission that holds the shifter pawl and its spring in place. After a long ride or when the transmission is even slightly overfilled with oil, it's not uncommon to see a streak of oil that has dripped out the breather hole.

Clutches also began to slip, and at first, Guzzi thought the problem was that the clutch springs were too weak because they updated them to heavier parts, according to a service bulletin dated May 24, 1967. Unfortunately, the real problem was leaky clutch pushrod seals that sometimes allowed transmission oil to migrate forward along the pushrod and onto the clutch plates. On V700s up to 2715, the seal was just a felt tube over the clutch pushrod. Later machines received a new plastic sealing tube, along with a new throw-out-bearing assembly to replace the failure-prone early assembly. Updated parts included the caged bearing, inner and outer bearing carrier bodies, clutch pushrod, and pushrod seal. Unfortunately, these parts didn't really work much better than those they replaced, so they were updated once again, at a later, unspecified engine number.

New Fork

A revised front fork was introduced at the same time as the throw-out bearing and seal. According to Ivar de Gier, the change was made to make it more stable when fitted with the Guzzi fairing. Updated parts included the top nuts, top and bottom yokes, and fork-tube shrouds.

Intake Reducer Bushings

If you ever have a chance to look at the intake port on a V700, you'll probably come to the conclusion that it was designed for a carburetor much

larger than the 29-millimeter Dell'Ortos fitted to the production machines. The result is lousy low-speed engine response. According to Dave Hewitt, "People would crack the throttle open, and the things would spit back through the carburetor and die." In an attempt to fix the problem, Guzzi began fitting what they called "reduction bushings." These are metal sleeves that slip inside the intake port, all the way to the valve stem, reducing the diameter of the port for higher intake velocity. Each bushing's mounting flange is sandwiched between two thick gaskets, which isolate the carburetor from cylinder-head heat. Because two gaskets are used with the reduction bushings, the metal manifolds also had to be shortened to maintain the proper spacing between the carburetors and the airbox. There is no record of when the bushings were first used, but Hewitt remembered that they were offered as a kit to retrofit to earlier machines.

New Rocker Covers

The rocker-box covers were given a makeover for a sleaker, more modern appearance starting with machine number 3120. On the new cover, the company name was moved from the large flat atop the cover to the raised oval boss near the top's inboard edge. Three fins were added atop the cover, more for embellishment than cooling. Best of all, the tunnels for the mounting screws were made equal in length, getting rid of the appearance of warts suggested by the hex heads of the four long screws formerly used on each cover. All eight mounting screws for each new cover were short Allen-head types (instead of eight chrome-plated hex-head bolts, four long and four short). This same basic cover, with slight modifications for breather lines and in various states of polish, would be used on Guzzis until new valve covers were introduced on the Convert in late 1974.

New Pulley with Four Timing Marks

Although the V700 engine was designed from the start for easy serviceability, this quality was further improved when Moto Guzzi began fitting a new lower generator pulley with four timing marks instead of one. There is no record of when the new pulleys were first fitted, but the revised timing procedure for using the new marks was first explained in a service bulletin dated October 14, 1968. This revised pulley would also be used on the following V7 Special and Ambassador models.

Coil-Bound Valve Springs

At some unrecorded time during the V700 production run, Moto Guzzi began fitting valve springs made of larger diameter wire. Unfortunately, they didn't revise the length of the springs or any other associated parts, so the springs would occasionally become coil bound, according to an undated bulletin, which states, "If you find any that are coil bound, please advise immediately so compensating top collars can be forwarded to you immediately." None of the dealers the author spoke to recall this problem or were even aware that the wire diameter had changed, so it was likely a very rare problem.

LAPD Guzzis, Part I

In 1967, the Los Angeles Police Department (LAPD) had a larger fleet of motorcycles than any other police force in the world. Not only that, but they were looked to by hundreds of smaller forces around the United States as the trend-setters in police motorcycles and equipment. In the world of police motorcycles (called "motors" by the motorcycle policemen, who refer to themselves as "motor officers") in the 1960s, having the endorsement of the LAPD was like having the endorsement of Michael Jordan for basketball gear. The Berliners and Moto Guzzi looked on the endorsement of the LAPD as one of the keys to making Moto Guzzi a household name in America.

Bob Blair of ZDS Motors (the West Coast distributor) and Mike Berliner carefully mapped out their strategy. Blair sent his best salesman to make the first pitch. According to Steve Zabaro: "We had a red-hot young kid salesman named George Kerker. He didn't like the police much, but he could sell like a son of a bitch." Kerker convinced Ray Wynn, a civilian engineer who was in charge of motor vehicles for LAPD, to at least look at the new Guzzi.

Wynn was fairly impressed with what he saw, but there wasn't much he could do because new machines have to be tested and budgeted for, and it was too late to accomplish all that in time for the next bid cycle. With visions of hundreds of potential future

sales in mind, Blair made Wynn an offer he couldn't refuse. According to A.J. Lewis, Blair's shop foreman, "Blair was gonna give two to them to try out, but the law doesn't permit that. He said, 'We'll take care of them. All you have to do is run them, and they'll cost you $1 each.'"

So began the LAPD-Guzzi saga, and so ended the first year of the V700.

1968 V700s

Moto Guzzi was never too concerned about making distinctions between "year models," preferring to make changes whenever it was convenient, and often without even notifying its dealers, let alone advertising the improvements. Thus it was that the full-page ad from 1967 was reprised in U.S. magazines with only a new headline and the attention-grabbing and ever-so-informative "Many refinements for '68," without listing a single one.

Undoubtedly, some of the changes and improvements listed earlier occurred during 1968, but the author couldn't find documents to conclusively prove this, so they are listed all together. Several dealers I spoke to only remember two visible changes for 1968: a rubber gaiter to cover the wheel end of the front-brake cable and thinner black pinstripes around the tank panels. Apparently, the Guzzi painters had finally perfected the technique of masking for a clean edge around the chrome panels, so they no longer needed a 1/4-inch-wide stripe to clean up the panel edges. The new stripes were about half as wide, giving a neater appearance than previously.

For the European market, the V700 was substantially revised late in 1968. White was the standard paint color, and these revised V700s were fitted with 29-millimeter Dell'Orto concentric carbs,

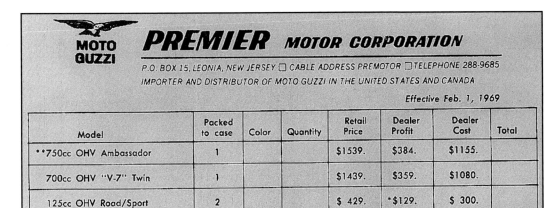

An original price list from early 1969 shows that both the V700 and new Ambassador were available.
Mike Berliner

MOTO GUZZI

PREMIER MOTOR CORPORATION

P.O. BOX 15, LEONIA, NEW JERSEY ☐ CABLE ADDRESS PREMOTOR ☐ TELEPHONE 288-9685
IMPORTER AND DISTRIBUTOR OF MOTO GUZZI IN THE UNITED STATES AND CANADA

Effective Feb. 1, 1969

Model	Packed to case	Color	Quantity	Retail Price	Dealer Profit	Dealer Cost	Total
**750cc OHV Ambassador	1			$1539.	$384.	$1155.	
700cc OHV "V-7" Twin	1			$1439.	$359.	$1080.	
125cc OHV Road/Sport	2			$ 429.	*$129.	$ 300.	
125cc OHV Scrambler	2			$ 469.	*$141.	$ 328.	

All Prices Port of Entry East Coast or West Coast   Single Case $5 - Add'l.

Except V-7 $15.00 additional for West Coast.   * 30% Profit

*** Date of Availability will be announced at Daytona Time.*

This sales flier from Premier Motor Corporation shows the first-series Ambassador. These machines were basically "punched-out" V700s—same gas tank, side-bowl carbs, and usually even the small-valve heads of the V700. They were primarily sold in the United States. *Rick Mahnke/MG Cycle*

a rectangular taillight like those used on the prototypes, a revised seat (with integral grab strap and the company name across the back in white letters), and the bike was fitted with a Bosch starter. Inexplicably, U.S. models (through the early Ambassadors in 1969) were fitted with the side-bowl carbs and Marelli starter.

Apparently, though, at least some white ones were brought to the United States. According to Torello Tacchi: "Some [buyers] shied away because of the color, so Mike finally got some in at the end of '68 with some nice paint jobs, some nice white ones with stripes and stuff." Midwestern distributor John Gregory got his first white V700, with matching fairing and bags, in the summer of 1968 and kept it for himself. To dress up the one-color machines, more pinstripes were added. The striping schemes used on these machines is complex. See the early-Ambassador color illustration for details.

Later still, but again at an unspecified date, Moto Guzzi began fitting revised SSI carburetors, now with accelerator pumps, and the pumps were made available to customers to retrofit to their bikes. An early reference to the feature was in a service bulletin dated September 10, 1968, that advised when starting the machine not to "tickle V7s with accelerator pumps." Typically, the new feature wasn't advertised until many months after it was in use. The hot modification at the time was to remove the intake reducers and add the accelerator pumps.

In January 1968, *Cycle World* published its first road test of the civilian V700. The magazine liked it, calling it a "huge, magnificent touring twin." The only major criticism was reserved for the petcocks, which aren't marked for the on and off positions, and which cause the carbs to overflow if left on when the machine is parked. The British magazine *Motorcycle Mechanics* also tested the V700, a U.S. model, in the United States, because there was not yet an importer in Britain, according to the magazine. The editors liked it, commenting that it was at least the equal of the BMW and that "unlike the BMW, the Guzzi draws crowds of admirers."

LAPD Guzzis, Part II: The First Test

After the initial flurry of activity to get the new V700 into dealer showrooms, the Berliners and their agents began to seriously court police departments in 1968, according to Heinz Kegler: "We did a big promotion to police departments, LAPD and New York City in particular."

By January 1968, LAPD had taken delivery of its first $2 worth of Italian heavy metal: two repainted V700s, with white tanks and black fenders and other bodywork, according to Kegler. Kegler had vacationed over the Christmas holidays in Albuquerque, New Mexico, and was to go from there to Los Angeles to show the LAPD mechanics the fine points of Guzzi maintenance: "We talked with their chief mechanic and demonstrated the technical part of the Moto Guzzi versus the Harley—maintenance, chain drive versus shaft drive, ignition timing, valve adjustment, how to pull the engine out, even things as simple as changing a tire. They were very, very impressed."

Some of the motor officers also looked at these two Guzzis as a sign of good things to come. According to former motor officer Gary Smith:

Being a rider of English bikes, I was desperately hoping that they would find something to replace the Harleys because they were big turds. If you've only ridden a Harley, like some of those old motor cops, you have no way to judge what other motorcycles are about. The old-timers who just puttered around giving tickets to old ladies who jaywalked in Fairfax, they don't need a bike that you can maneuver at high speed.

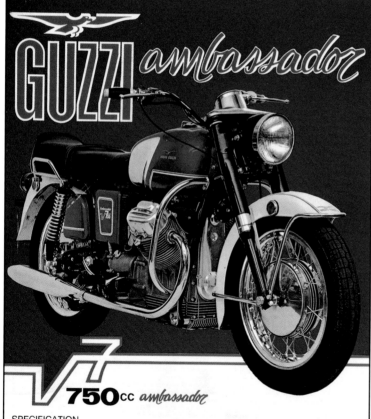

GUZZI *ambassador*

√7 **750**CC *ambassador*

SPECIFICATION

ENGINE: 750 cc OHV twin, air cooled, alloy barrels with hard chrome lining, light alloy hemispherical heads, steel con-rods with thin wall bearings, anti-friction main bearings (as used in all F 1 Race Cars)

BORE: 83 mm

STROKE: 70 mm

BRAKE HORSEPOWER: 55 HP SAE at approx. 6500 r.p.m.

COMPRESSION RATIO: 9 to 1

FUEL TANK CAPACITY: 4¹/₂ US gallons

LUBRICATION: wet sump, gear type oil pressure pump

CLUTCH: twin plate dry clutch with cushion drive

SUSPENSION: telescopic front fork with two-way hydraulic suspension. Rear swinging arm with hydraulically damped 3-way adjustable shock absorbers

DRIVE: shaft drive with dual bevel gear to the rear wheel

FRAME: duplex tubular structure. Center and side stands

BRAKES: large diameter twin leading shoes front brake. Single LS rear brake

WHEELS: 18'' alloy rims

TIRES: 4.00 x 18'' front and rear

SEAT: large dual seat with chrome hand rail, safety bars

SPEEDOMETER: Borletti car type speedo instrument (oil pressure gauge, neutral indicator, and charge indicator)

ELECTRICAL SYSTEM: 12 V 300 W battery powered system. 6'' 45/40W headlight Electrical starter

The LAPD ran the two machines in tests for most of that year, and were mildly impressed. They liked the V700, but found it lacking in performance, especially when encumbered with a windshield, footboards, and the usual police equipment, which added both weight and aerodynamic drag. In fact, so encumbered, the V700 was hard-pressed to keep up with the Harley, which had a 500-cc displacement advantage over the Guzzi. Former motor officer Ron Brian remembers the V700 as being "pretty weak." The sentiments of the police echoed those of the American dealers: "We need more power!" The Guzzi engineers who attended the dealer meetings made careful notes of the wants of Guzzi's largest export market and began work on satisfying the unsatisfiable.

Even though the LAPD liked the V700, getting them to include the Guzzi in a formal test and bid process was considerably more difficult than getting them to buy a pair for $1 apiece. First of all, though LAPD had taken a few foreign machines into the pipeline for testing in the past, none had made it even to the bidding process. Policemen tend to be very conservative; most of them liked their Harleys and looked on the foreign machines as too small and too delicate for real police work. There was also the perception among the police hierarchy that they would open themselves up for criticism if they bought foreign machines. Even so, all of them knew that Harley had been selling them the same machine for over a decade and would never improve it without some serious competition.

The first task was to get invited to the formal tests. Ray Wynn, notwithstanding some of the good reports about the Guzzi, stonewalled when approached by Bob Blair. Finally, Mike Berliner flew to California to lend a hand. Blair and Berliner arranged a meeting with Ray Wynn and Jack Wood, an influential motor officer. Here are Berliner's recollections of the meeting:

Jack Wood and Ray Wynn were 100 percent against buying the foreign machines and didn't even want to test them. Jack Wood was 100-percent Harley—then he changed his mind after he rode Moto Guzzis for a while. Eventually, he went to work for Bob Blair selling Moto Guzzis to police departments.

I said to them, "I was in the U.S. Army and I am an American citizen. I am paying my taxes and duties to the U.S. government on every single motorcycle and component that comes in. Bob lives in California. He pays his taxes to the state, so we're entitled to a fair shake from you people." Ray Wynn said, "What do you mean?" I said, "What I mean is very simple. Here is my honorable discharge from the U.S. Army and the papers saying I am paying my taxes, so I want you to test my machines. After you test them, you can tell me you don't like them, but at least test them." Ray Wynn looked at me and said, "You know, you have a point there, Mr. Berliner."

LAPD motor officer George "Scotty" Henderson testing a prototype police Ambassador at the first formal LAPD trial for the Moto Guzzi, in November 1968. Not used to the power characteristics and weight distribution of the Guzzi, Scotty nearly looped the "Goose" on his first dragstrip run. This is perhaps the first Ambassador brought to the United States. *Scotty Henderson collection*

That done, the next step was to have "the latest equipment" (a favorite phrase of Mike Berliner) to show the LAPD. The test criteria specified that the machine must be submitted with all the necessary police gear, that it do the quarter mile in 16 seconds at not less than 80 miles per hour, have a top speed of at least 90 miles per hour, and many others. Not too demanding, certainly, but the V7 could just make a 16-second quarter mile in civilian trim; it would have no chance with police gear, so they needed one of those 750s that the factory was supposedly working on in response to demands for more power. Although Berliner doesn't remember bringing over any special machines for the test, someone clearly did.

Motor officer George "Scotty" Henderson supplied the author with a photo of himself launching off on a dragstrip run at the first test in November 1968 (the photo was dated by the processor). The bike he is on is a prototype 750 Ambassador with the large gas tank that didn't appear on production Ambassadors until about midyear 1969. It has all the police lights and gear, and Scotty is about to learn a lesson about the "Goose" as police officials, Blair, Berliner, a Guzzi engineer, and a Guzzi test rider look on:

I had never ridden a Guzzi before, only Harleys. I got up to the line, gave a big handful, and let my hand off the clutch. I started out fine, but pretty soon, I'm looking straight down the track, but the darn tank's right in front of my face. I almost went over backwards on the darned thing. I mean it was straight up in the air. If that had had the same kind of throttle [without a throttle return spring] as on the Harley, I'd have flipped it. On a Harley, when you give it a big handful, it just spins rubber like a car; the front end doesn't come off the ground. You get on a Guzzi and do the same thing, it's like there's Velcro on that rear tire; the front wheel goes straight up in the air because there's so much weight on the rear wheel.

American dealers insisted on louder mufflers with a larger opening than on the V700 prototype and on European models. Those mufflers are featured in this ad, which also hints at the availability of the 750-cc Ambassador.

After that near disaster, an Italian test rider, reportedly Luciano Gazzola, took over for a few runs to show Henderson how to keep the front wheel down. "Then, Scotty practiced a few times and was able to keep the wheel down on the rest of the runs," according to motor officer Herbert C. "Pinkie" Meredith, who was also there that day.

Henderson liked everything but the brakes: "Of course back in those days, none of the brakes were very good," he recalled. "You'd get in a pursuit and after you went around four corners and had to use your brakes, you were on your own. If the car would stop for you, you'd go right on past him."

When the testing was over and the police were comparing clipboards, the Italian rider, tired of watching everyone else have all the fun, put on a show. According to Mike Berliner:

> He climbed on one of the Moto Guzzis and roared off around the track. When he got near the police, he stood up on the seat and held his arms out to the sides as he rode past for about 150 feet. I can still see him up there—a good-looking guy, red cheeks. The police loved it. A couple of them were of Italian descent, and they yelled, "Bravo!" and ran over to shake his hand.
>
> The engineer was a little bit upset. He said, "Why did you do this?" The rider said, "Aaahhh, it's such a beautiful track, and the weather is so beautiful!"

Joe Ballister, supervisor of maintenance and training for LAPD, remembered, "He was standing on the seat with his arms out, leaning way forward. I thought, my God, the guy's going to go over the front wheel."

The Guzzi had passed the test, so Blair and Berliner were free to bid. But the trials were not yet over. The police still had some concerns about comfort and needed the ergonomics and controls made as similar to the standard controls on the Harley as possible because a motor officer might be on a Guzzi one day or a Harley the next. After Blair submitted his bid, the LAPD agreed to buy 10 Moto Guzzis as an experiment, but only if the comfort problems could be solved.

1969 V700s

The V700 was back for 1969, in the traditional red-and-silver and in the relatively new all-white and all-black. The only visual differences for the year were phased in gradually. As old stocks of fenders dried up, new fenders were fitted that had a hole in each side for mounting the U.S.-spec side reflectors that were to be a new feature of the forthcoming 750 Ambassador. On most machines, these holes were filled by a small rubber plug. Later, some were fitted with the reflectors.

The third major U.S. motorcycle magazine, *Motorcyclist*, got around to reviewing the V700 in its January 1969 issue. The test V700 lacked the accelerator pumps, but the editors loved it anyway and were quite impressed with its performance, commenting that "One of our lighter test riders was able to lift the front wheel a good foot in the air during our acceleration test every time he shifted from first to second." They also liked its handling, saying, "This is one big bike that handles more like a scrambler than a grand touring machine."

The only announced update for 1969 was what an ad in the February 1969 *Cycle World* called "FUEL INJECTORS, a Guzzi exclusive!" As you can probably guess, the Guzzi wasn't fuel-injected; rather the ad trumpeted the accelerator pumps that had been introduced in the latter half of the previous year.

Late Police and Military V700s: 1969–1978

Moto Guzzi sold V700s to police and military forces all around the world. These V700s were painted whatever colors were requested by the force ordering the machines. After production of the Ambassador began, production of civilian V700s was effectively halted, but the V700 was still available as an inexpensive police and military machine, officially through 1976. Many were sold around the world, especially to third-world countries in Africa, Asia, and South America, but also to some municipal police forces in Europe, according to Ivar de Gier.

These machines weren't time capsules, however, frozen at the 1969 configuration. As updates were introduced to the Ambassador and Eldorado, some were also made to the police V700s; examples include larger gas tanks, five-speed transmissions, four-leading-shoe front brakes, 850-style crankcases with "waffle" reinforcements, and even the twin-instrument dash, on special order. In essence, some of these late V700s were Eldorados with the 700-cc engine. A wide range of police equipment was also available, including Hollandia sidecars, fairings, windshields, leg shields, bench seats, special lights, panniers, and so on.

According to de Gier, the last V7s were produced in 1978 for Dutch municipal police forces. Some of these were sold on the civilian market while new, and for very low prices. When Moto Guzzi learned of these unauthorized civilian sales, the company at last deleted the model from the catalog.

First-Series Ambassadors: "Punched-Out" V700s

Although word had been leaking of a new, larger Guzzi for some time, the first official word about it in the United States wasn't published until about the time the machines arrived. In his "Report From Italy" column in the March 1969 *Cycle World*, Carlo Perelli reported that displacement was bumped to 750 cc, power was increased to 60 horsepower, carburetors would be Dell'Orto concentrics, top speed was increased to 112 miles per hour, and quarter-mile times had dropped to 14 seconds. It also mentioned that Lino Tonti was already at work on an even more powerful version. The U.S. version of the new 750 was named "Ambassador." According to several dealers, the moniker was coined while flying to Italy on one of TWA's "Ambassador" flights. (Mike Berliner remembers that the name was coined by his P.R. man, Walter von Schonfeld.)

No one seems to remember exactly when the models debuted, but a clue is provided in Scotty Henderson's report of his trip to Italy. In March, he was at the Berliner headquarters in New Jersey, where he was introduced to Michele Bianchi (by this time the commercial director of Moto Guzzi) and Lino Tonti (chief engineer of Moto Guzzi), who were there for a "motor showing." Early March then is a likely date for the introduction of the new model to the dealers.

The first 750s in the United States were really nothing special. "When the 750s came out," remembered dealer Torello Tacchi, "they were nothing but a 700 punched out. Same tank and side-covers, paint job, small valves and carbs. Even right-hand shift on the very first ones."

Externally, the only things decidedly new were the "Ambassador V750" transfers on the battery covers, a recontoured seat (this seat is essentially the same as the seat introduced on late-1968 European V700s), and a new color option: metallic red with white fenders. Paint and striping on the all-white

To sort out the last concerns of the LAPD about police Guzzis, motor officer Scotty Henderson was flown over to Italy to suggest changes to the police machines. He is shown here on one of the police prototypes. At far left is George Kerker, a sales rep for West Coast distributor ZDS Motors. Third from left is Mike Berliner, U.S. importer for Guzzi. At far right is Lino Tonti. *Scotty Henderson collection*

and all-black machines generally matched that used on the late V700s in those colors.

Internally, the bores had been increased to 83 millimeters, for a total displacement of 757.5 cc. This increase in displacement required new cylinders and pistons (still with four rings, but the lowest [oil] ring had been moved from the piston skirt to above the piston pin). Guzzi rated these first-series Ambassadors at 55 horsepower (five more than for the V700, but five less than for the second-series Ambassadors that would soon follow).

Even these little-changed machines had a positive effect, however. Though first-series Ambassadors weren't a great deal more powerful than the V700s, which many dealers still had on the floor and which they could still order, these early Ambassadors did have a noticeable increase in torque over the V700. And they looked more modern, especially sitting side-by-side with a red-and-silver V700. "In order to help us sell those V700s," remembered dealer Ken Johnson, "they [Premier] took back the red-and-silver parts and sent us some white parts."

Apparently, all these first-series Ambassadors were shipped to the United States. The planned 750 for the rest of the world would be called the V7 Special, and wouldn't debut until later in the year.

LAPD Guzzis, Part III: Scotty Beams Down in Italy

Wanting to quickly resolve the final hurdles to making the Guzzi acceptable to the LAPD, Bob Blair and Mike Berliner decided to send an LAPD officer over to Mandello del Lario to show the Guzzi engineers and technicians firsthand what needed to be changed. The natural choice of who to send was Scotty Henderson, the man who had

Henderson spent an afternoon in high-speed testing on the track at Monza. He is shown here on the police Ambassador at center. George Kerker is shown at right. *Scotty Henderson collection*

done the bulk of the testing in the November trials. Scotty's main goal? To make the "Goose" more like the "Hog."

According to the report Henderson wrote after the trip, he arrived with Mike Berliner and George Kerker in Milan on the morning of March 5, 1969. The entourage from America was met by Guzzi employee Reggie Allas in his Camaro and a motorcycle escort of two factory riders. They checked into a hotel in Milan and got right to work.

Henderson looked over the machine that had been prepared for his test and saw that some of their earlier requests had been met—a Harley-type sidestand and relocation of the ignition switch to a position under the seat—but there were still some changes needed, including individual marks for each mile per hour and a resettable trip odometer for the speedo, a shorter rear brake lever, and so on.

Henderson wasn't finished and back to his hotel until 11:00 that night, but the Moto Guzzi personnel stayed up all night making his requested changes so he could test ride it the next day. When Henderson arrived, they were just finishing. He took it for a ride at 10:00, accompanied by a factory rider so he wouldn't get lost, and they rendezvoused with the "factory heads" for lunch at a place near the Swiss border. Afterward, they rode back to the factory, made more changes, and headed off for more testing on the racetrack at Monza.

At Monza, Henderson put on about 30 miles, testing for top speed, acceleration, shifting, brakes, and siren operation. It was far from an ideal testing location. He recalled that "Everybody and everything was on that track—cars and motorcycles. I'd be honking around there going about 100 miles per hour, and a race car'd go by doing 160. It scared the shit out of me." It was after dark before the testing concluded.

A few days later, after the bike had been modified to his liking, Henderson and a test rider took off for Rome on their motorcycles, followed by Reggie Allas, Michele Bianchi, and George Kerker packed in Allas' Camaro. Once on the toll freeway, the test rider kept pushing the pace, averaging about 95 miles per hour. Even so, they spent most of their time in the slow lane. "You didn't dare get in that left lane if you weren't going fast," Henderson remembered. "Those Ferraris and Maseratis would get right up behind you and honk their horn. You'd look back at 90 miles per hour, and these cars would be six feet behind you. They wanted to go 120."

Eventually, they made it to Rome where they spent the day taking pictures at the Coliseum, St. Peter's Square, and other sites. They also met with officials of the Rome police department, the Corazzieri, and the Ministry of Internal Affairs.

By the time he left Italy the next day, Henderson was fully satisfied with the new Guzzi, and his

Henderson rode the police prototype to Rome for a day of meetings with government officials and for photos. Note the extra cable to the front brake mechanism. It connects to a device near the top half of the brake arm. This is probably a brake-light switch. *Scotty Henderson collection*

report, which concludes with, "Anything we want, they will comply with," eased the mind of Ray Wynn, and the sale went forward, with 10 new Ambassadors being delivered to the LAPD in May.

NYPD and Atlanta PD

Also mentioned in Henderson's report was the fact that the Berliners were preparing two batches of police motorcycles at that time, for the Atlanta and New York City police departments. "Thanks a lot," Berliner said to Henderson. "It is the LAPD's fault that I have to change all the shift levers to the other side! Everything the LAPD gets, all the other departments want." According to Atlanta dealer Beno Rodi, Atlanta took a batch of about 50 V700s at first. A photo he provided shows them to be white with the Italian police fairing.

Second-Series Ambassadors

When the second-series Ambassador came in, it proved to be just what customers had been asking for: more power, bigger gas tanks, and modern looks—all for only $100 more than for the V700. Better yet, its performance increased far beyond what a simple 54-cc jump in displacement would suggest, and the surprising level of performance made the Ambassador the first true realization of what the Berliners wanted from the beginning—a big, fast, all-around road machine.

A letter dated August 8, 1969, from the service department at Premier at least tells the number range of the new-style Ambassadors:

Looking uncannily like impish comedian Pee Wee Herman in one scene from the movie, *Pee Wee's Big Adventure*, a member of the Corazzieri, the presidential guard, poses with Scotty Henderson in Rome. The V700 is one of the first series for the unit, with the deeply valanced fender and extra-large crash bars. *Scotty Henderson collection*

In order that we should fill your parts orders correctly, we ask you to state the following when ordering parts for the 750cc Ambassador:

Whether the engine number is in the 1200 range or the 1300 range. The difference between the 1200 and the 1300 range is very recognizable, of which you are aware. The 1300 range has the new-type tank and concentric carburetors, etc.

Externally, the larger gas tank was the most prominent change. Its capacity is 5.84 gallons (22.5 liters), and the graceful outline of the new tank harmonizes well with the overall front-heavy look of the machine. Its filler cap is still hinged and has a lever on top to release the cap, but the lever pivot is now in the center of the cap itself. Slightly different pinstriping schemes were used, depending on the color (see the color brochure). Similar to those on the first-series Ambassadors, tanks on all-white machines also have a large black panel on top, with red-and-black pinstripes around the panel. Red tanks and black tanks have only the pinstripes tracing the panel.

To accommodate the new gas tank, the frame was stretched by about an inch at the steering head and was reinforced by a new gusset on each side. This change stretched the wheelbase from 56.9 inches to 57.8 inches. The forks were basically the same as on the late V700.

The engine on the Ambassador was substantially new and beefed up to handle the extra power and torque of the larger displacement. New parts include the crankcase, crankshaft, pistons, cylinders, oil-pump relief valve, and cylinder heads. The

crankcase had updated webbing reinforcements to better resist cracking. Cylinders had an 83-millimeter bore with chrome-plated cylinder walls. Pistons were made in A, B, and C sizes to optimize clearance within the bores. The oil pump was uprated to operate at 54–60 psi (rather than 35–42). Bowing to the Ambassador's lack of ground clearance, three steel rails were added to the bottom of the sump to serve as a skid plate.

New cylinder heads fitted to the Ambassador helped take advantage of the added displacement by increasing breathing ability for an increase of 10 horsepower, from 50 to 60 (compared to the V700), according to factory figures. Although the size and volume of the combustion chamber remain the same, bigger valves (41 millimeters intake and 36 millimeters exhaust) and new valve guides (now retained by a circlip) were fitted. These larger valves are controlled by a nested spring pair and new steel collar (replacing a single spring per valve). Also, a revised plug was added to cover the access hole to the top stud of each cylinder.

The other big boon to performance was the new (new for U.S. models, same as used on non-U.S. late-1968 and 1969 V700s) 29-millimeter Dell'Orto concentric carburetors with accelerator pumps. These carburetors are simpler, easier to tune, less prone to leaking, and give better overall carburetion. Even though intake reducer bushings were not used on the Ambassador, two thick spacer gaskets were fitted between the carbs and cylinder heads.

The Ambassador used an almost identical four-speed transmission as that of the late V700. Functionally, the major change was to a much stiffer, square-section spring on the cush drive. Also new was a redesigned fill plug and an adjustment screw on the clutch arm to compensate for wear in the clutch plates.

Because of the increased power and torque of the 750-cc engine, overall gear ratios were raised by revising the rear-end ratio from 8/37 (pinion/ring-gear; 4.625:1) on the V700 to 8/35 (4.375:1). The new gearing was housed in the same basic rear drive case as used on the V700.

Controls on the Ambassador were revised to feature a conventional left-side toe-shift pedal (replacing the heel-and-toe rocker pedal; sometime later, the heel-and-toe shifter was again fitted to the Ambassador), right-side rear-brake lever, and a starter push-button on the right handlebar (the ignition switch isn't wired for actuating the starter from the switch). The handlebars have a slightly different bend than those on the V700 and are mounted to taller handlebar risers. Serrations added to these new bars make for a more secure mounting to the risers.

The backing plate for the rear brake was also revised. On the new plate, the brake-cam pivot was moved to the three o'clock position (from the 12 o'clock position on the V700), and the lever attached to the cam was also new and was mounted up (rather than down, as on the V700). Also introduced was a stouter tie rod for linking the backing plate to the frame.

Other parts changes on the Ambassador included a revised taillight mount, a new headlight bucket that is shorter in overall length, a steering-head lock, larger diameter shock mounts, stainless-steel spokes, an easier-to-use centerstand with longer "feet" that extended rearward only, a one-piece plastic generator cover, and "waterproof"

shielded spark-plug caps. New fuel petcocks were also fitted.

With three standard color schemes, riders had real choices about the look of their new machines. In white, the Ambassador looked large, clean, and stately. In black, it looked a bit trimmer, and more classical in style. In red and white, it looked brighter, sportier, and more modern. All three were popular, but some dealers did better with a particular color than with any others. Said Seattle dealer Bob Budschat, "Everyone wanted black with white striping because they looked like a luxury touring

George Kerker tested several prototypes on the track that day, like this faired version. While at Monza, he learned a few tricks that he later applied to his ZDS racing Ambassador. After leaving the employ of ZDS, Kerker founded the high-performance exhaust manufacturing company that bears his name. *Scotty Henderson collection*

On June 26, 1969, Lino Tonti took two specially prepared and lightened V7 Ambassadors/Specials to Monza to contest world speed records. Despite numerous problems with tires shedding great hunks of tread, numerous records were set. Tonti returned with the bikes in late October to set even more records. *Moto Guzzi*

bike." Oddly, another Seattle dealer, Jerry Drager, sold more white than any other color. Mike Harper, owner of Harper's Moto Guzzi in the Kansas City area, noticed a completely different preference among his customers: "If you had one of those pretty red-and-white ones on the floor, people just gravitated to it."

First Reviews

The second-series Ambassadors were in the United States in time to be reviewed in the October 1969 issues of *Cycle World, Motorcyclist,* and *Cycle*. All three magazines loved the way the Guzzi was transformed by the increased displacement and restyle, concluding that it was better in every way than the V700 it replaced. *Cycle World* said, "If Roman gods rode motorcycles, the Moto Guzzi would surely be the choice of Bacchus. It is a big, stylish, and strong road machine that reeks of luxurious plenty; a genuine ultra-bike." Even its already pleasant feel seemed improved, *Cycle World* concluding that at idle it was like "sitting on a large water buffalo with a grumbling stomach."

All were especially surprised at the improvement in performance. *Cycle* ran the Ambassador through the quarter mile in 14.36 seconds, compared to 16.1 seconds for the V700. *Cycle World* didn't quite match that quarter-mile time but commented that, "Second gear shifts brought almost a foot of daylight between front tire and pavement, while third gear chirped the rear tire." *Motorcyclist,* which tested both the civilian model and the heavier LAPD model, commented on the latter that "for a big scoot, the thing goes like whoopie. In first, it'll burn rubber till you let off the go valve, and in second, it will wheelie just like the pretty red-and-chrome model."

With reviews like these and the obvious good looks and performance of the machine, Premier had good reason to increase its advertising presence, which it did starting in the September 1969 *Cycle World*, with a two-page ad showing the Ambassador and listing its signature features. Guzzi's U.S. sales began a quick rise that would soon make the United States Guzzi's biggest export market.

LAPD Models

Taking advantage of all its work on modifying its new Ambassador for the LAPD, Moto Guzzi made it available through its dealer network to whoever wanted one. This model was basically the same as the bikes delivered to the LAPD, meaning that it was fitted with footboards, heel-and-toe shift pedal, a speedometer with individual marks for each mile per hour, a revised instrument console with various switches and four warning lights (also, generally, a plug covering the hole for the ignition switch), ignition switch on the left side below the seat in place of the left toolbox, higher risers and handlebars, solo saddle with springs at the rear, left crashbar with a mount for the Harley-style sidestand, rear crashbars, a twist-off gas cap, tubular guards around the cylinder heads to keep officers' boots from burning, turn signals, a front brake-light switch, and an electrical switch on the right handlebar to control the radio and flashing lights. Surprisingly, *Motorcyclist,* which reviewed both the civilian and a fully equipped LAPD model in its October 1969 issue, liked the police version better, commenting that "The combination of solo seat, footboards, and long, swept back 'sit up and beg' bars makes for one of the most comfortable riding motorcycles we've sat on for quite some time."

Record-Setting and Racing Ambassadors

What!? you might say; a touring bike setting speed records?

Yes, in the right hands, any machine can be made fast, and when those hands are as talented as those of Lino Tonti, even a slug like the Ambassador can be massaged to set world records. During the spring and early summer of 1969, Tonti and

Luciano Gazzola had developed and tested a pair of very fast Ambassadors that they hoped would set some speed records. One machine had a reduced bore of 82 millimeters to bring its displacement down to 739.2 cc (according to a Moto Guzzi ad) so it qualified for the 750-cc class, and the other was left at its stock 757-cc displacement for the 1,000-cc class. Both had a compression ratio of 9.6:1, revised gearbox ratios, and 7.9-gallon (30-liter) fuel tank, and both were lightened to 347 pounds (158 kilograms) by removing shrouds and covers, the generator and starter, fenders, lights, and anything else that wasn't essential.

In June, they took the machines to the track at Monza in search of the world's 10-km, 100-km, 1-hour, 6-hour, and 1,000-km records, the first serious speed trials Moto Guzzi had made since 1957. First, famed racer Remo Venturi took to the track.

Rounding a bend, his rear tire began to break up at over 129 miles per hour. He was able to get the machine stopped without crashing, but he was so shaken by the experience that he just walked away from the machine and left the trials. Even so, he had already broken the 10-km record at 130 miles per hour and had run one lap at 138.5 miles per hour.

Angelo Tencani took the same machine out (after a tire change, of course), and the new tire failed, too. After another change of tires, he climbed back on and set a 100-km record and the record for 1 hour, both at 130 miles per hour.

The smaller machine set records, too, despite tire problems of its own. However because of the tire problems, Tonti called the record runs off before contesting the 1,000-kilometer and 6-hour records.

These successes were trumpeted in an ad in the October 1969 *Cycle World*, with the subheadline "Remo Venturi streaked down the Monza straights at speeds of 145 miles per hour on a production Guzzi V-7."

Not satisfied with the records, Tonti and Gazzola developed the machines further and took them back to Monza in October with more power (65–68 horsepower, thanks to a redesigned camshaft, pushrods, and intake tract) and tires Tonti had confidence in, to contest the previous solo

This Premier sales flier shows all three colors available on the Ambassador—all-black with white striping, all-white with red and black striping, and red-and-white with white striping on the red parts and black and red striping on the white fenders. Note that the red and black stripes on the all-white Ambassador's tank are different thicknesses and never actually merge together. Shown are the second-series Ambassadors, with the larger, reshaped gas tank, larger-valve cylinder heads, and Dell'Orto concentric carburetors. *Rick Mahnke/MG Cycle*

Officer Gary Smith, one of the original 10 LAPD motor officers assigned Guzzis in 1969. Smith called the group the "Goose Patrol." These motor officers proved the Ambassador on the mean streets of L.A. By 1970, LAPD police Guzzis were a common sight and provided an incalculable amount of free advertising for Moto Guzzi. *Gary Smith collection* records again, but also to contest the similar sidecar records. Gazzola was scheduled to ride on some of the record runs. Unfortunately, he broke his leg a short time before the date of the runs while testing a prototype 850. Despite this setback, the Guzzi crew broke all its previous records and set new ones on the sidecar rigs, too.

On October 30, the 6-hour and 1,000-km runs were made. In the 1,000-km run for the 750-cc class, the team of Brambilla, Bertarelli, and Pagani broke the world record with an average speed of 125.5 miles per hour (202.5 kilometers per hour) and the 6-hour record with an average speed of 125.3 miles per hour (202.1 kilometers per hour). During these runs, a rocker arm broke, and it was replaced within 7 minutes. After that run, the team of Mandracci, Patrignani, and Trabalzini broke the 1,000-km world record for the 1,000-cc class with an average speed of 129.1 miles per hour (207.9 kilometers per hour) and the 6-hour world record with an average speed of 110.6 miles per hour (177.9 kilometers per hour). During the latter part of the 6-hour run, the transmission failed, but it was replaced in 40 minutes. Because of breakdown, the last part of the session had to be ridden in the dark—on a bike that didn't carry lights.

The next day, many more solo and sidecar records were broken, despite such problems as broken sidecar mounts. As on the day before, the last record laps were set in the dark. In all, 19 new

records were set over the two days. The secrets to turning an Ambo into a world-beater? "Meticulous preparation of capacity, power, and handling," according to Tonti.

One of these record-breakers actually made it to the States, where it was owned for several years by Dave Hewitt. Hewitt sold it to Dale Bedeaux in Minneapolis, Minnesota, owner of Carl's, a Norton, Ducati, and Guzzi shop. Bedeaux used it for display in his shop and even rode it occasionally, never matching the performance Tonti got out of the machine. "I could never believe that thing set world speed records," he remembered. "We could never get it up much over 120 miles per hour—and we were young and foolish, so we tried." After a few years, mechanics at the shop began scavenging parts off it, and eventually it was dismantled. The engine was sold for a street Ambassador, and the rest of it was scattered and lost over the years. Truly an ignominious end to a glorious machine.

Reno Leoni also saw some speed potential in the dowdy Ambassador and carefully prepped one for a four-hour endurance race in Danville, Virginia. Limited by class rules for production machines, modifications were minimal—straight intake manifolds and removal of the stands—but careful preparation and assembly kept the bike in one piece through the whole race while faster Honda fours, Norton twins, and Triumph triples broke down and fell out. Leoni and Dick Cassetta piloted

This interesting racer was built by George Kerker from a wrecked Ambassador, with sponsorship from Bob Blair of ZDS Motors. Kerker took it to Daytona in 1970, but was disqualified from competing by the AMA, which hastily constructed a V-block that all motorcycles had to be able to pass through to compete. The Guzzi's cylinders prevented its passing through the block. Rider Phil Terranella is shown on the machine on August 8, 1971. *Dave and Sharon Hewitt collection*

Another Ambassador custom painted by its owner. The color choice is certainly striking, if not factory-correct. Like this Ambassador, some came fitted with new-style battery covers along with the single-instrument nacelle. Later Ambassadors, and all V7 Specials, were fitted with a dual-instrument cluster.

the machine to victory. "We were like the turtle, and they were like the hare," he said. But this triumph of the hare was no fluke. Leoni and Cassetta also won the endurance event at Summit Point, West Virginia. After this victory, Leoni retired his leathers and went on to tune some later Guzzis that were decidedly less turtle-like.

The team of Al Phillips, Torello Tacchi, Bob Waitfield, and Jonathan White raced a 1971 Ambassador at the 24-hour endurance race at Mosport in 1971. The only modifications to the machine were straight intake manifolds, velocity stacks, and "a couple of Coke cans" to replace the stock oil breather box, according to Tacchi. "We took the lead about the eighth or ninth hour, and just sat in front until about 5 or 6 hours before the end. Then, the plug cap shook to pieces and destroyed the core of the plug. We tried to pull it out, but the threads began to strip, so we pulled the heads, drilled the spark plug out, and put another plug in." By the time they got back on the track, they were in third, and that's the place they finished. They would be back the next year, however.

Clearly, the Clark Kent Ambassador, with a quick change of clothes, had the potential for Superman-like performance. "The Ambassador was a really under-rated motorcycle," said Tacchi. "With just the straight intakes and velocity stacks added, that sucker topped 120 miles per hour, and we were driving that thing at valve float all the time. I eventually sold the motorcycle to a friend of mine, and he kept it for seven years. It never gave him a lick of trouble."

LAPD Guzzis, Part IV: The "Goose Patrol" and Wally Maxwell

The LAPD sought to give its 10 new Moto Guzzis a fair test by assigning them to a hand-picked group of officers, according to Gary Smith, who was among this group, which he nicknamed the "Goose Patrol":

There were several of us who were approached about riding the Guzzis because we were younger, more aggressive motor officers who weren't so affected by a stigma that existed then, and still exists today, that "We don't want to ride those damn foreign bikes." They picked a group of guys that they thought would give them a good test.

On the street, most of the Goose Patrol loved their new mounts. The Guzzi's good handling even saved the officers the pain and indignity of a few spills. Gary Smith remembered one in particular:

One day, it had started to sprinkle, just enough to make the street slippery. I was in the left-hand lane chasing this car. I started coming up on him too fast, and hit the rear brake. Of course, the rear wheel skidded out. I let off on the brake and the wheel came up. I then just tapped my brakes to keep from going down while the car pulled over. I finally got stopped and barely tipped my front wheel on this guy's bumper after sliding the rear wheel out four times. If I'd have been on a Harley, I'd have been thrown on my ass the first time.

The V7 Special was the non-U.S. equivalent to the Ambassador. Like later Ambassadors, all V7 Specials came with dual instruments and new-style battery covers. Specials and Ambassadors differed mainly in paint, decals, and pinstriping. Some Specials were fitted with the round taillight shown, but most had a rectangular taillight, like that used on the second-series V700s introduced late in 1968. *Moto Guzzi*

The Guzzis also proved unusually reliable. The only serious problem was with the rear drive case cracking. According to former motor officer Ron Brian, the pinion gear would ride up the ring gear and break the case under certain conditions, which happened to him twice:

> One morning I went off Olympic Boulevard onto Union Avenue to chase some guy that was flying along Union. When I went around the corner and jumped down into second gear, I popped the case. The car pulled over and I coasted up next to this guy, and he didn't know that my bike had just broken. I told him to pull across the street and stop at the curb, so he did. You shoulda seen the look on that guy's face when I had to push the bike across the street and all the oil was streaming out the back end. He was thinking, "Shoot! I coulda just taken off."

The Guzzis were also stealthy compared to the loud Harleys the LAPD normally used. According to Brian, "You'd go down the street and you'd sneak up on people and could get 'em before they knew you were there."

The verdict after the test? Thumbs up. If Blair submitted a competitive bid, the LAPD might soon be a big Goose Patrol.

And Blair made the right move toward that goal. Realizing that it takes a cop to sell to cops, he hired former LAPD cop Wally Maxwell, who had worked with Ray Wynn in the Motor Transport Division, to shop the Guzzi around to police departments around the Western states.

The first deal he closed was for the 10 LAPD Guzzis; then he approached Long Beach. Representatives of that force met him at the marina, and he described what happened:

> I pulled the bike out, and one guy made a crack: "Which end does the spaghetti come out of?" I kinda laughed, and told them to try it first, because it's a hell of a bike.
> I thought they were going to just do some figure eights and other stuff, but the first thing they

wanted to do was drag with one of their Harleys—right at the marina. I was really worried, because the Goose wasn't like the Harley. If you revved the Harley and let out the clutch, it would just spin the rear wheel like a car and take off. If you did that with the Goose and weren't careful, it'd come right over on top of you. The guy riding the Goose must've known what he was doing, though, because he whipped that Harley good. After the run, a training sergeant turned to me and said, "You just beat our fastest Harley." I said, "I didn't know I came here for a race."

After that, Long Beach bought, and Maxwell took the Guzzi wherever there were police bikes, making sales in Phoenix, Tucson, Riverside, San Diego, Oakland, and in many other towns and cities.

1970 Ambassadors

For the start of the 1970 model year, the Ambassador was essentially unchanged. As the year progressed, a few subtle refinements were introduced, such as small clamps that wrap around the header pipes and attach to the crashbar lower mount to reduce header-nut loosening, and the reintroduction of the heel-and-toe shifter. Very late in the year, a third series of Ambassadors began entering the United States. These updated machines had the dual-instrument console, updated battery covers, and key locks on the toolboxes first used on the V7 Specials sold in Europe.

The new battery covers extend further to the front, completely covering the airbox and have a column of horizontal louvers in the front half of the cover. Front and rear edges are essentially square, making the Ambassador's midsection even portlier looking than it already was. New decals are used on these covers, reading "V750" over "Ambassador" in script. These new covers first appear in the Premier ads in the December 1970 *Cycle World,* so they may not have made their debut until the 1971 model year.

The new instrument console was a great improvement. It featured a tachometer for the first time—a useful addition, even for a touring machine. The console itself was an aluminum casting with a center-mounted ignition switch, two warning lights to each side, the tachometer far to the left, and the speedometer far to the right—all mounted atop the fork. One great feature of the new panel is the flip-up cover to keep rain out of the ignition switch. The panel is finished in a nonglare, black wrinkle paint. The new console and instruments first appear in the Premier ads in the May 1971 *Cycle,* so they may not have made their debut until the 1971 model year.

An October 1970 addition to the parts book shows that Bosch starters and generators began to be fitted to Ambassadors. Although rated at 0.5 horsepower (versus 0.7 horsepower for the Marelli starter), the new Bosch starter proved to be a more efficient starter than the Marelli, because the Bosch's solenoid switches down to half its power draw once fully engaged, leaving more battery power available to the starter motor itself. The Bosch generator also required fitting of unique pulleys and a specialized Bosch voltage regulator.

The V7 Special

While the Ambassador was intended solely for the American market, some second-series Ambassadors (concentric carbs and large tank, but with V700-style battery covers) were delivered to other markets for homologation, magazine road-testing, and initial sales, according to Ivar de Gier. In late 1969, the official European version of the 750 was released, called the V7 Special. It is basically the same as the third-series Ambassador with the new instrument console and the longer battery covers, except that the speedometer reads in kilometers per hour, from 0–240, and the shifter is on the right.

The V7 Special also received slightly different paint and pinstriping. The standard color for Specials was white, but some special colors may have been used on request of the individual importers.

Most V7 Specials were fitted with a rectangular taillight similar to the one on the prototype and late European versions of the V700, but photographs of test machines of the day show that some of these bikes had the round light fitted to U.S. machines. Also, the V7 Special was fitted with a replaceable-bulb headlight with a pilot bulb, while Ambassadors had a sealed-beam bulb. Most were fitted with the Bosch starter and generator, rather then the Marelli units.

A review in the February 1971 *Motorcycle Mechanics* characterized the V7 Special as something of a two-faced beast: "Dr. Jekyll, so suave and unpretentious, can be changed into a ravenous beast of a road-burner by cracking the whip and *driving* the thing." It also mentioned that at last there was a British importer, D. H. Barrett Motors, and that the price was £962. Another review was in the October 1971 *Motorcycle Illustrated.* The reviewer, Dave Minton, loved the Guzzi's comfort and "the leech-like way the monster stuck to a line on a fast bend." He summed up the V7 Special as a bike "built for men who have within them the love of truly great machines, and an urge to travel. A long way. Fast."

With the V7 Special came more sales to police departments within Italy and in other countries. According to Enrico De Vita, who was then Moto Guzzi's export manager, he was able to sell V7 Specials to all the major police forces in Italy. In addition, he sold them to police forces in Sweden, France, Yugoslavia (50 to Tito's personal guards), and many others around the world.

LAPD Guzzis, Part V: Maxwell Makes the First Big Sale

After the first 10 Ambassadors had proved themselves with the Goose Patrol, Wally Maxwell worked up a bid that won an order for 85 new Ambassadors. On May 4, 1970, the first 40 were delivered, and another 45 on May 27, according to figures provided by Nate Thibodeaux of the LAPD. To get them all set up and in service quicker, Bob Blair had the LAPD mechanics come down and use his facilities. According to Frank Ortiz, a mechanic for the LAPD, "He gave us his facility, and we set up two shifts to put these machines together for the police department. The city paid us for doing the work, but Blair offered to pay us for working over-

The new Bond may ride a BMW, but the *real* Bond, Sean Connery, rode a Guzzi, at least on this day in March 1971, during the filming of *Diamonds Are Forever. Moto Guzzi*

European markets. It was basically a police Ambassador, with a few special parts to make it look even more like a Harley, most notably a seat that was almost a perfect knock-off of the mid-1960s Harley buddy seat, complete with black top and white sides and a chrome grab rail around the back. Also part of the package were high buckhorn bars, footboards, rear crashguards, a Harley-style windscreen, small saddlebags, and chrome-plated fenders. Most lacked the left toolbox, having the ignition switch mounted in its place. Some Californias may have been imported into the United States. If so, they apparently were fitted with the police solo saddle, rather than the black-and-white saddle of the Euro version, according to U.S. parts books.

Though the Ambassador continued to sell well, it was facing new competitors such as the /5-series BMWs and some late hardware from Japan, so Moto Guzzi was readying the next stage of its big tourer, with more of what its customers were asking for—displacement and power.

LAPD Part VI: Let the Wobbling Begin

Jack Wood proved as adept as Wally Maxwell had been. He sold the LAPD 50 more Ambassadors, which were delivered on May 3, 1971. In addition, more and more police departments began to sign on for Guzzis, including the CHP, which finally bought four for evaluation, according to the remembrances of some CHP officers, backed up by a report in the June 1971 *Cycle World.*

With so many police bikes being pushed out the door, it is inevitable that a few lemons would be among them and that it would be a difficult task to keep up with all the spare parts required. This was proving to be the case in late 1970 and 1971. Some machines exhibited a tendency to weave at high speeds—not many, "probably a half percent" of them according to Steve Zabaro. These machines were typically returned to ZDS, where they were checked to see if there was mechanical cause. Seldom was any found. The real problem was the rearward weight distribution caused by all the radios and bags, combined with the dubious aerodynamics of the police windshield. One incident, in particular, pointed out that the problem was something that needed to be addressed.

A bike was returned by the City of Orange to be checked. Enrico De Vita, Moto Guzzi's export manager, was at ZDS, so he personally examined the machine, working all day to try to pinpoint the cause of the wobble. Unable to do so, he took it out for a ride that evening, with Steve Zabaro following on another police machine. According to De Vita, as they were nearing the end of the freeway, at a speed of 87 miles per hour, the bike went into a wobble that only got worse as he slowed down. Here's what Zabaro saw:

time or pay us to work on our own time to get them done faster."

And Maxwell soon proved so successful at selling to other police departments in the West that ZDS Motors was at times hard-put to keep up with orders. According to shop foreman A.J. Lewis:

> We'd set up big batches of motorcycles—lights on 'em, test 'em, get 'em all ready to where the cop could just step on 'em and go. Then, we'd load 'em on big 40-foot flatbed trailers we had all rigged up here at Glendale. We had drivers that would drive these big rigs wherever they had to go. Truckloads and truckloads of 'em, especially to Arizona.

Unfortunately, Maxwell and Blair had a falling out in the spring of 1970, and Blair hired another former LAPD officer, Jack Wood, to take over police sales. Wood also proved adept at his job, and police sales continued to increase.

1971 Ambassador, V7 Special, and California

By the start of the 1971 model year, the design of the Ambassador and V7 Special had stabilized into what would be their final form, with the dual instruments, locks on the toolboxes, and the square battery covers. A new throw-out bearing was introduced during the year, according to a technical bulletin dated January 7, 1971.

In late fall 1971, a new version of the 750, called the California, made its debut in several

All of a sudden, he goes into a wing-ding. I mean this thing's hitting the steering stops, his feet are up in the air, way off. All of a sudden, he falls down. Sparks were flying, pieces of radio and saddlebag were flying by me. He came to rest in the middle of a lane. I got stopped and dragged him to the shoulder. He was hurt, all skinned up.

De Vita spent two and a half hours in the emergency room to repair extensive abrasions. He was then flown to Italy, where he spent another month in the hospital.

After the crash, the bike was returned to Italy, along with two other wobblers, where they were test-ridden and studied. Unfortunately, an Italian test rider was later killed on one of them, according to Ivar de Gier. From this point on, ZDS took no chances. When the distributorship received a wobbler, it replaced the bike with a new machine and dismantled the old one for parts, destroying the frame.

1972 Ambassador and V7 Special

For the start of 1972, the Ambassador and V7 Special returned as Guzzi's flagship touring machines, joined by the new V7 Sport, which is covered in the next chapter. Both Ambassador and V7 Special were essentially unchanged for the new year, except that the last batch was built with some parts that would soon debut on the 850 Eldorado, most notably the new-style engine case with "waffle"-pattern reinforcement webbing.

Enter the Eldorado and 850 GT

Moto Guzzi released a new flagship touring bike in early 1972, the 850-cc Eldorado for North America and 850 GT for the rest of the world. The early Eldorado and 850 GT differed from one another mainly in cosmetic details and headlights. Also available were the police version of the Eldorado and the California version of the GT, which were basically 850-cc versions of the similar 750-cc models of the previous year, except that they were fitted with new-style slash-cut mufflers and safety cutouts wired into the neutral switch and/or the clutch cable. Some California versions may have been imported into the United States for 1972, but most dealers say they did not enter until 1973 or 1974, and in very limited numbers. If so, they apparently were fitted with the police solo saddle, rather than the black-and-white saddle of the Euro version, according to U.S. parts books.

The 850 Engine

Given the design limits placed by spacing of cylinder studs on the V7 engine and the need to make the new engine as reliable as previous engines had been, the only practical way to increase the engine's displacement was by increasing stroke. Lino Tonti and his staff thus designed a new crankshaft with a throw of 78 millimeters instead of 70 millimeters. More stroke was also the key to increasing engine torque, and torque is more important for a touring engine than is horsepower. Even with the

Sales rep Dave Hewitt sits on an Ambassador police bike that is being crated in Mandello del Lario. His wife, Sharon, is shown to his right. *Dave and Sharon Hewitt collection*

The third-series Ambassador went on sale in late 1970 or early 1971. It featured dual instruments, the new-style battery covers, and locks for the toolboxes.

750cc GUZZI AMBASSADOR

The Machine Built Exclusively For Unlimited Touring.

stroke increase, the 850 Guzzi engine was still over-square, at 83x78 millimeters.

Completely redesigned pistons drove the new crank. Although of the same 83-millimeter diameter as the Ambassador pistons, the Eldorado pistons have a lower deck height and dome, and a more conventional three rings (instead of four). These pistons also increased compression ratio from 9:1 to 9.2:1.

To handle all that new torque without cracking, the crankcases were greatly reinforced with new webbing on the outside of the case, in a "waffle" pattern. Use of an engine-number prefix began with the 850, which was given the "VP" code. A revised distributor with a separate base/mounting bracket was also fitted, so the case was also revised to accommodate the new distributor. Automatic advance range of the Eldorado distributor was the same as that used on the Ambassador (28 degrees), but static timing on the 850 engine was reduced to five degrees (versus 10 degrees on the 750), so total advance on the 850 was also less, 33 degrees versus 38 degrees. A new lower pulley for the generator belt was fitted, with repositioned marks to reflect the new timing.

Five-Speed Transmission and New Rear Drive

The five-speed transmission was similar in design to the old four-speed, but was essentially all-new, from the new case with "waffle" reinforcement webbing on the outside to all the shafts and gears

inside. The rear drive was also new, with a stouter case (left "as cast" except for a polished side panel), a deep sump with removable pan, and 4.625:1 gearing (same ratio as on the V700).

Electrics and Other Small Changes

All Eldorados were fitted with the police fuse boxes in the headlight shell, giving several extra terminals for accessory circuits and an extra set of fuses. The new machines were also wired for turn signals and had a new switch box on the right handle-bar to control the turn signals. Another spin-off from the police bikes became standard on all civilian models: a brake-light switch for the front brake, mounted inline in the cable. (This may have become standard earlier, on the 750, but most Ambassador wiring diagrams do not show a circuit for the switch.)

Also new were two yokes that link the header pipes to the lower downtubes of the frame. These consist of two metal stampings with a pinch bolt in the center. In a move to save money, Moto Guzzi stopped polishing the valve-cover castings with the last of the Ambassadors. Police bikes received an unsprung solo seat and larger, seamed mufflers.

Paint and Graphics

Except for the new engine and transmission and some minor changes to the battery cover and toolbox graphics, little was changed in the transition from Ambassador to Eldorado and from V7 Special to 850 GT.

Color combinations on the Eldorado are the same as offered on the Ambassador: all-black, all-white, and red and white. Standard color combinations on the GT included all-black, metallic red, and metallic green, but custom colors were available for about $50 extra, according to David L. Smith (European correspondent for MGNOC), who bought a new GT directly from the factory in 1972. The first GTs had chrome panels on the sides of the tanks, but later in the year, the panels were painted over. On the GTs and on California versions of the GT and Eldorado, the fenders were usually (but not always) chrome plated.

First Reviews

All these changes made for a torquier, more powerful motorcycle that was less prone to detonation and was just as stately and reliable as the old 750—no mean accomplishment, and testament to the excellence of the Guzzi design department under Tonti. Rated power was 64 horsepower, only four more than the 750, but the increase in torque was far more substantial than that.

The first magazine road test in the States was by *Motorcyclist* in June 1972. They loved the increase in performance, commenting that it made an already good touring bike into a great one. *Cycle* tested it for its July issue and loved it, too, calling it "550 pounds of rolling grace" and declaring it "the most comfortable and least tiring tourer on the market." *Cycle* also found the big Guzzi's performance side, turning a quarter-mile time of 14.04 seconds, which was "as quick as any Triumph Bonneville we've ever tested." The only real complaint either magazine had about the Eldorado was the brakes, which were not up to the standard of the disc brakes fitted to some other machines of the era.

Eldos in the USA

With the advent of the Eldorado and its sporting sibling that year, the V7 Sport, Guzzi dealers were in the gravy. "Eldorados sold then like Harleys do now," according to distributor John Gregory. "We could sell every one we could get and not have

to discount them a dollar." During the Eldorado years, Premier sold as many as 5,000 big Guzzis a year, according to Enrico De Vita. While that total may not seem so impressive when compared to the sales of Honda or Kawasaki, it was not far off the number of Harley FLHs sold in some of those years, and is more than Guzzi's total production in some years in the late 1980s and early 1990s.

Tranny Recall

The Eldorado wasn't all good news, however. Its new five-speed had problems. In fact, the first 1,500 were recalled and repaired for free in a depot set up by the Berliners in New Jersey, according to a July 18, 1972, letter from Premier. This recall was no huge burden if a dealer had sold only four or five such bikes to local customers, but it was another

The 850-cc Eldorado made its debut on the U.S. market in 1972 and was an instant best-seller. The Eldorado chassis is basically the same as that of the late Ambassador, but fitted with a longer stroke engine for a displacement of 844 cc, a five-speed transmission, new "waffle"-pattern ribbing on the engine and transmission cases, and a new rear drive housing with an integral sump. This tattered original Eldorado is the author's favorite day-to-day ride.

All markets but the United States got the 850 GT instead of the Eldorado. This GT is a 1974 model, with four-leading-shoe front brakes, a fully painted gas tank, and police-style mufflers. Some 1972 GTs have twin-leading-shoe front brakes and chrome panels on the gas tank; most 1972 and 1973 GTs have torpedo mufflers. *Moto Guzzi*

matter entirely if the dealer had just sold 50 or 100 to the local police department. Even worse for those dealers, the Berliners paid only about $15 to the dealers for removing and replacing each transmission, a fact some of the dealers are still bitter about to this day.

What was the problem? The lock ring holding mainshaft fifth couldn't handle the thrust load and would sometimes break, allowing the gear to jump out of place and lock up the transmission. How did this happen? "A mistake in the interpretation of the production of a shaft," according to Lino Tonti. The solution? According to Jonathan White of Domi Racer, "They drilled a hole in the shaft at the root of the spline and inserted a spring and plunger to lock the inner race in place so it couldn't turn and it couldn't back off, and the race was flanged to keep the gear on." This fix was also implemented on the production line during that first year (and is still in use today). Updated transmissions are stamped with the numeral "3" near the drain plug or near the speedometer cable connection. Other bulletins suggested that the flywheel bolts be updated to bolts marked "10K."

Shift return springs also were failure-prone on the early five-speeds, but a sturdier part was soon substituted on the production line.

The other major problem was with the rear drive, more specifically with the recommended amount of oil to be used in it. The new rear drive housing was designed with a level-plug location for the initial specification of 230 cc of gear lube. In a July 1972 bulletin, Moto Guzzi revised the recommended quantity to 2 1/3 pints, about a liter, which is way too much. This was corrected in an August 30, 1972, bulletin to the correct 350 cc. An August 15, 1973, dealer bulletin describes an L-shaped metal pipe that could be attached at the level hole to raise the level to the correct 350 cc. After Moto Guzzi had used up whatever quantity of housings was in stock, they began fitting a new housing with the level plug raised to indicate 350 cc.

De Tomaso Buys Moto Guzzi

With the success of the V700 and following models, Moto Guzzi was recovered enough that IMI began entertaining buyers for the company. Several parties started negotiations to buy the company, including Gilera and the Berliner brothers (who had earlier tried to buy Ducati, and their plans for Moto Guzzi included setting up production in Mexico to build models for the United States), but all these negotiations came to frustrating ends because a deal had essentially been struck behind the scenes for sale of the company to Benelli (which Alessandro De Tomaso had bought a controlling interest in the previous year).

Apparently, however, it was no ordinary deal, and questions about the subject seemed to make interviewees noticeably nervous. In fact, only one would discuss the deal on the record, former Moto Guzzi employee-turned-journalist Enrico De Vita. According to interviews with De Vita and an article he wrote for the June 1976 *Quattroruote*, Benelli paid 1.25 billion lire for Moto Guzzi on December 21, 1972. De Vita estimated the value at five billion lire.

Sweetheart deal? Seems like it, but wait 'til you hear the rest.

According to De Vita, a curious transaction also occurred on December 21, just before Benelli took over: IMI transferred three billion lire into Moto Guzzi's coffers. Result? In one stroke, De Tomaso took control of Moto Guzzi, was paid back his purchase price, and pocketed 1.75 billion lire for his trouble.

Now, there are many possible explanations for this sudden influx of funds—scheduled transfer of operating capital, payments received from motorcycle sales, or more nefarious ones—but the timing certainly raises suspicions.

De Tomaso quickly asserted control over Moto Guzzi, pushing out many of the senior managers, paring down the engineering department, and making plans to combine the efforts of his two motorcycle companies. For better or for worse (and there are compelling arguments for both points of view), Italy's oldest motorcycle company was now in the hands of the Argentinean former race-car driver.

1973 Eldorado and 850 GT

The Eldorado returned with few changes, and most of those were all in the transmission. The layshaft was updated to allow sleeves with wider flanges for first through third gears and the horseshoe-shaped bearing retainers for the front of the input shaft and the rear of the layshaft were updated to a new design that fastened with three bolts instead of two. The transmission case and rear cover were also revised with a boss and threaded hole for the third mounting bolt. Late in the year, some Eldorados were imported with a four-leading-shoe front brake. In the United States, Premier began selling the Police Special, which was basically the police model (which a civilian could order through his dealer), but with the regular dual seat of the civilian model. It was available in black, white, and two-tone paint schemes, according to *Cycle* magazine's buyer's guide in 1973. Accessory manufacturer Wixom Brothers also began selling package Eldorados that came fully outfitted with Wixom fairing, saddlebags, and rear trunk, for $2,189.

For the world market, the 850 GT and California were updated with a four-leading-shoe front brake and revised paint schemes.

Changes During the Year

A few refinements were made to the 850 engine during the year. Connecting rods, bolts, and nuts were strengthened for more secure mounting of the bearing caps to the rods. And in an economy move that made the Guzzi engine even more like an automotive engine, the timing gears were replaced by a timing chain, tensioner, and sprockets. The oil pump was also revised as part of the switch to the timing chain. This change took effect starting with engine 58532. Unfortunately, the chain didn't prove as reliable in operation as the gears had

been, mostly because chain life depended greatly on maintaining proper tension through fairly frequent manual adjustment, and most owners didn't bother. Also, the pad on the tensioner wore rapidly or disintegrated entirely on some machines, accelerating chain wear.

A.J. Lewis' Hot-Rod Eldorados

Sales to police departments around the United States continued with the advent of the Eldorado. The LAPD took delivery of 16 on April 20, 1973, and the CHP finally made a quantity purchase, estimated at 70 by several CHP personnel. Many smaller departments such as New Orleans and the Dallas Airport Police also bought Eldorados.

Even with the additional power provided by the 850-cc engine, many LAPD and CHP officers still wanted more, so the ever-helpful A.J. Lewis, shop foreman for ZDS, came to the rescue with a 1,000-cc kit that he would install for favored officers. "That 1,000 cc was awesome!" Lewis said. "It was scary; unless the guy was a good rider, he had no business being on one." The need for such power? "If an officer's sitting alongside the highway, and some guy in a Corvette comes by at 100 miles per hour, he might have to run five miles to catch up. But with this Moto Guzzi 1,000 cc I'd build, he'd jump on that freeway and catch that sumbitch before he got down the road a mile."

These officers would bring in their machines, ostensibly for some routine fix, and A.J. would

DEPENDABLE MOBILITY
FOR PATROL, ESCORT OR PURSUIT

850 POLICE SPECIAL

In the United States, sales to the police market sometimes approached the quantity sold to the civilian market, so many of Premier's ads and brochures featured the police bikes prominently. *Dave and Sharon Hewitt collection* punch out their bikes to 1,000 cc and hot-rod them. He had L.A. Sleeve make the custom iron liners and Venolia forge the pistons. Before assembling the engine, Lewis polished and flowed the heads and put in a modified V7 Sport camshaft. He was also careful to keep all the stock parts in a special box with the officer's name on it so he could

return each bike to the stock displacement and tune before the officer had to trade in for a new motor.

Another interesting police machine entered testing during the year, a version of the 850 GT that was fitted with an automatic transmission, according to an article in the October 1973 *Motorcyclist*. Some of the former officers interviewed

An original former-CHP Eldorado. This Eldorado is rare for U.S. models in that it has a four-leading-shoe front brake. Most U.S. Eldorados had twin-leading-shoe front brakes. A few with the four-leading-shoe front brake were imported in late 1973 and early 1974. Later 1974 models had single-disc front brakes.

for this book recalled seeing the machine, but none of them remembered it vividly. The rest of that story is in the next chapter.

1974: Disc-Brake Eldorados and 850 GTs

Production began in November 1973 of the final version of the Eldorado and 850 GT, with a completely new front end that, at last, after even Harley-Davidson had introduced the feature, included a disc front brake.

The new forks fitted to these machines were similar to those used on the V7 Sport, meaning that they had unpainted aluminum sliders, internal springs, and cartridge dampers so they were lighter and had real damping action for the first time. These new forks required a revised front fender and fender stays.

The new forks and brakes transformed the handling and braking ability of the Eldorado. Because of the too-large piston diameter of the master cylinder, lots of hand pressure was still required for quick stops, but the action of the disc was much smoother and more powerful than even the four-leading-shoe front brake, without the latter's tendency to self-servo.

The only other major change for all machines that year was the switch from the old, round taillight to one that was more rectangular. This taillight went on to serve on many Guzzis until the mid-1980s. Late in the year, some Eldorados were fitted with Marelli electrics in place of the Bosch electrics.

Amal Carbs

Some Eldorados and GTs came fitted with what many considered a curious substitution of parts: 30-millimeter Amal concentric carbs in place of the 29-millimeter Dell'Ortos. To adapt these carbs to the Guzzi required special manifolds, air-box rubber, throttle and choke cables, and various other small parts. Most dealers thought the Amals were a disastrous change and wondered why Guzzi would switch to carbs of dubious reputation when the local product had been working so well. Torello Tacchi summed up both issues well: "Some said it was because of a strike at Dell'Orto, and some said the factory did it for performance reasons. All I know is that when we did get the damn things, we had to take 'em off because they used to leak and piss all over. They had a little more performance because they were 30 millimeters, a little larger than the Dell'Orto 29s, but they weren't very good carburetors. You had to prime them, and they leaked. And of course, some customers didn't like them because they weren't pure Italian." According to Umberto Todero, the Amals were fitted in response to some requests for them, some originating in the United States.

The Last of the Police Eldorados

Both LAPD and CHP bought new Eldorados in 1974 and really liked the new disc-brake machines. According to Nate Thibodeaux, LAPD bought 11 of the new machines and took delivery on February 27. These machines were most likely seen as a test of the disc-brake machines. Clearly, they liked them because they placed another order for 131, which were finally delivered on May 22, 1975 (according to Thibodeaux), long after the model was officially discontinued.

According to the recollections of CHP officers Chuck Downing, Fred Moeckley, and Larry Piatt, Moto Guzzi won the entire bid for 1974, which they estimated to be for 90–120, some of which had a four-leading-shoe front brake and some of which had a disc.

A Brief Reprise

In its final year, the Eldorado remained a phenomenal seller. Most dealers were out of new machines long before the selling season was over and began crying for more. Very few of the new 850-T models were available, so Mike Berliner did the best he could to get more new machines, eventually scrounging up "a few hundred" 850s from Europe in late 1974 and early 1975, according to Jonathan White, whose Domi Racer distributorship bought most of these GTs to sell to its dealers. But these machines were not exactly what the dealers expected. When the crates were opened, inside were 850 GTs and Californias, most with Amal carbs and four-leading-shoe or disc front brakes, and in a weird variety of colors, including metallic green, salmon red (almost pink), and brown, in addition to black. Although these machines were rare, there are still some around. Joe Eish was offered some of the GTs to sell in his dealership, Eish Enterprises, which is still selling Guzzis. He declined to buy them because he thought the Eldorados were still

The 850 California was basically a police version of the Eldorado (floorboards, speedo-only dash, ignition switch in place of the left toolbox, rear crashbars, windshield, high bars, Harley-style sidestand, and so on), with a few special civilian parts, such as Harley-style buddy seat, chrome fenders, saddlebags, and rack. Most Californias had four-leading-shoe front brakes, but some late ones came with a single front disc brake. The California was sold mostly in Europe, but some were imported to the United States, usually with a single seat in place of the buddy seat. *Moto Guzzi*

Like many police Eldorados, this CHP model has the ignition switch mounted on the left side, in place of the left toolbox. The 16-inch rim at the rear is CHP spec.

available. That turned out to be a mistake; when he needed more Eldorados, they were all gone and he had to sit with an empty floor for six months because of a delay in getting enough 850-Ts.

The word among American dealers and distributors was that Alessandro De Tomaso despised the Eldorado and saw it as a remnant of the old Moto Guzzi that should be done away with as soon as possible, even though it was Moto Guzzi's top seller by a wide margin. Worries over wobbling and other handling faults probably added impetus to the decision to replace the venerable tourer with a new machine, the 850-T. But in the opinion of many, De Tomaso may have made a rash decision that, at least in the United States, cost the company dearly. "There was nothing wrong with those last Eldorados," said John Gregory. "With the new forks, disc brake, and Metzeler tires, they tracked straight as a string, as fast as you want to go. De Tomaso kinda shot himself in the foot on that one."

Between new competition in the form of the Honda Gold Wing and the lukewarm reception given the new 850-T, Moto Guzzi lost the sales momentum the Berliners and their dealer network had worked so hard to build. It was the beginning of a long decline for Moto Guzzi in the United States because, according to Dave Hewitt, "Many of the Eldorado guys never bought another Guzzi. Some of them that stayed with Guzzi bought an automatic or a T3, and many of those went back to an old Eldorado. Eventually, many of them went to Gold Wings. I traveled the same territory for 27 years. I knew the dealers and the retail customers by face if not by name, and I kept up with what they rode. When we didn't give them what they wanted, they all moved on." In a fond nod to the Eldorado, the most successful American dealers of the coming few years succeeded largely on their ability to make their new-style Guzzis look like the old.

Left
Many Eldorados were dressed like this one before they even left the showroom floor. The aptly named "Miss Piggy" fairing and huge bags and top trunk completely change the character of the Eldorado.

CHAPTER 2

THE TONTI-FRAME ROUND-HEAD TWINS
V7 Sport through 850-T4

Compared to the dark days of the mid-1960s, Moto Guzzi was riding high at the dawn of the 1970s. Problem was, its success was based on essentially one model, the V7 Ambassador/Special, a heavy grand tourer that was already beginning to look old in a rapidly changing marketplace that included many newer and sportier machines, including the Honda 750 four-cylinder and the new /5 touring line from BMW. Speed records and superb sales in the United States and elsewhere notwithstanding, it became clear that the company needed to update its big twin for the new decade and expand its line-up to try to win over the sporting crowd if there was any hope of building on the sales momentum started by the V700.

Fortunately, such a machine was already in the works, the result of a little "bench racing" session on the sidelines at Monza in 1969, helped along by a little "fib" hatched on the same track early the next year. Before the decade was more than a few months old, the new machine would be seen roaring around the Mandello area, piloted by a swarthy dynamo of a test rider, Luciano Gazzola, or by a graying but spirited engineer with a cast on his leg, Lino Tonti, the machine's creator. This machine, the V7 Sport, was the start of a whole new model range for Moto Guzzi.

"Bench-Racing" Start

While the specially prepared Guzzi 750s were roaring round and round the Monza speed bowl in October 1969, breaking the records Moto Guzzi had set in June, Chief Engineer Lino Tonti, Managing Director Romolo De Stefani, and FIM President Dore Letto were discussing how Moto Guzzi could follow up the new records. Thoughts turned to competing in the 750-cc class of a very popular racing series in Europe—sport production—which had separate classes for standard production bikes and for factory prototypes.

To Tonti and the riders, it was obvious that the engine could be made powerful enough to compete, but it was equally obvious that the touring frame they then had was hopelessly tall and heavy and too "flexible" to serve as the basis for a successful racer. But frames are Tonti's forte, so he began forming a plan. During the discussion, De Stefani posited that the "perfect bike" would be capable of 200 kilometers per hour (125 miles per hour), weigh less than 200 kilograms (440 pounds), and have a five-speed gearbox. To Tonti, the speed records had been an interesting diversion from improving the production models, but this was starting to sound like serious fun!

Flush with the afterglow of many new world records set that day, De Stefani decided his idea for the perfect bike was worth spending some money on, and he gave Tonti the reigns. Tonti now had a mission and a mantra—"200 kilometers per hour, 200 kilograms, and five speeds"—and he was not the type to let such an opportunity slip. According to an interview published in the December 1997 *Ruoteclassiche,* Tonti had long chafed under criticisms that dubbed the Guzzi twin a "buffalo," and he was just itching to show the world what the old buffalo could do.

Breeding a Faster Buffalo

After the speed runs, Tonti began working on the new machine. Of course, the best way to realize his "perfect machine" would have been to start from a clean slate and design every part to meet "200 kilometers per hour, 200 kilograms, and five speeds," but Tonti had to be a realist. While the excellent sales of the big twins had put Moto Guzzi in a much better financial situation than it had been for many years, the company was still owned by a government agency, so to have any hope of getting his new project into production, Tonti had to achieve his goals with a minimum of new parts.

Though not the first of the Guzzi big twins powered by the round-head engine in the Tonti frame, the 850 Le Mans is arguably the most famous of all Moto Guzzis. The example shown is a 1978 model, which was essentially unchanged from the model's 1977 configuration.

To make 200 kilometers per hour, he needed to add about 10 hp to the 60 claimed for the Ambassador. To make weight, he had to cut about 66 pounds (30 kilograms). And to get five speeds, he needed to design a new gearbox (the same transmission the Eldorado/GT would later share). Most important was the need to make the new bike handle like a racer. To do this, he knew he needed an entirely new frame.

The basic goal was to build a better frame for use with a modified version of the existing engine. In this case, "better" meant stiffer and lighter, with more cornering clearance, and with lower overall height. "Stiffer" and "lighter" could be accomplished by a number of means, but the last two seemed to work at odds with one another because the only way to get more clearance with the same engine is to raise it higher in the frame, but if you raise that engine higher in the frame, you have to raise the overall height of the frame. The architecture of the Guzzi engine is what made both possible, except that one thing stood in the way—the generator. Unrestrained by the need for extra power to run police lighting, however, Tonti was free to get rid of that huge generator hogging all the space between the cylinders, which allowed him to raise the engine in the new frame.

That fall, Tonti tested the revised engine in a standard V7 Special frame and began the long

process of perfecting the design and getting more power out of the engine. The great challenge wasn't in getting another 10 horsepower out of the engine—he had done that and more for the speed-record bike—rather, it was in getting the power while simultaneously reducing its displacement to under 750 cc (from 757 cc) to meet displacement rules for 750-class racing, minimizing the number of expensive new parts, and keeping the famous Guzzi reliability.

Lino's Garage

Lino Tonti is an engineer of the old school, a man who can not only pen a great design but turn those sketches into metal all by himself. (Torello Tacchi, who worked with Tonti when the engineer came to the States for dealer meetings and service schools, called him "a tinkerer, a Thomas Edison."). Tonti has a well-equipped shop at home just for this purpose. Reportedly, he is also a man who treasures solitude when in the throes of creativity. Because of this, and to avoid interruptions in work caused by picketers at the factory gates during "hiccup strikes," Tonti retired to his home workshop at the start of 1970 to complete the design and build the first prototype frames. At home, he was also free to get assistance from Francesco Botta and Alcide Biotti, two former colleagues

Lino Tonti's V7 Sport made its debut in the production race at Monza in July 1971. Raimondo Riva is shown piloting the stock *Telaio Rosso* Sport (it even had lights, speedo, and tach in place) to a respectable third place behind a Triumph Trident (first) and a Honda 750 four-cylinder (second). Note that the tool-box cover has come open. *Moto Guzzi* from his days at Aermacchi (Aeronautica Macchi, originally a builder of aircraft).

This was not Tonti's first motorcycle frame. He had penned excellent frame designs for Bianchi, and for the Paton and Linto racers. He had also worked on airframe design while at Aermacchi, and these experiences formed his preference for straight tubes and triangulated structures. Together with his friend Botta, Tonti drew up his frame design, and Biotti helped with the actual fabrication. The frame that resulted was a masterpiece of straight tubes and triangles and was as compact as the architecture of the engine would allow. So tight is the engine wedged into the frame that it looks almost as if Tonti had built it of shrink tubing and stuck it in the oven to form fit itself around the cases. To the ever-lasting relief of *Guzzisti*, he made the lower frame rails removable. The new frame raised the engine up about 3 inches for added ground clearance while at the same time keeping the seat height about the same as that of the Ambassador. In sum, a low, stiff frame with good ground clearance and easy access to maintenance, hereafter known as the "Tonti frame."

Putting it all Together

With two prototypes of the new frame in hand, Tonti returned to the factory to get on with designing the rest of the machine, always with "200 kilometers per hour, 200 kilograms, and five speeds" in mind.

For an engineer of his talent and experience, turning the Guzzi four-speed into a five-speed was no great challenge. He kept the basic three-shaft design of the four-speed and basically just added a fifth gearset to the mainshaft and layshaft. Of course, there was more to it than that, including revised ratios on all the gears and needle bearings to replace the bushings on all the gears.

Weight savings came from slimming down everything that could be, including use of a small Bosch alternator, smaller Bosch starter, much lighter forks, slimmer fenders, and so on. Brakes were improved by basically doubling everything.

By early summer, the new machine was ready for testing, so Gazzola and Tonti proved the new machine on the streets and roadways around Mandello. Unlike most engineers, Tonti had enough trust in his own creations to climb aboard and wring them out. "I tested, assembled, and disassembled all the motorcycles I designed," he told the author. In fact, one day during V7 Sport testing, he lost control on a corner, and crashed. The bike landed on his leg, breaking it. Even that wasn't enough to keep Tonti off his new machine. He had the doctors set the leg with the knee bent far enough so that he could still ride and made a special mount on the machine to carry his crutches.

By the end of June 1970, the prototype V7 Sport was finished. By all accounts, Tonti got almost everything right the first time, so no significant changes were necessary before it was first put

A *Telaio Rosso*, one of the 200 or so special V7 Sports that were hand-built in the Guzzi experimental and racing department to homologate the type for racing. Everything about these early Sports (built in 1971) is special: frames are thin-wall chrome-moly steel, transmissions have special five-speed gearsets inside a non-ribbed case, crank and rods are mirror polished and balanced, heads are flowed, and so on. Even the swan-neck clip-ons differ from those later fitted to production Sports. *Moto Guzzi*

The great Mike Hailwood even tested the *Telaio Rosso*. According to test rider Luciano Gazzola, Hailwood had some difficulty with the right-side shift, as he appears to be having in this view. Moto Guzzi tried to hire Hailwood to race the Sport, but the company couldn't afford his fees. *Dave and Sharon Hewitt collection*

into production. Compared to the V7 Special and Ambassador, however, almost every part was changed in some way, and the machine that resulted looked long, light, lean, and low, as different from the old Moto Guzzi Ambassador as a thoroughbred race horse does from an ox.

The looks were no illusion. The V7 Sport prototype was an improved machine in every way, and it met all of Tonti's goals for weight, power, suspension, handling, and braking. In looks and performance, the V7 Sport was a true masterpiece, the equal of any motorcycle then in production. Truly, the only way to appreciate Tonti's creation is to look it over closely and then ride it. This book could easily be filled describing the clever attention to detail in every part, but that's not an option, so here are a few important highlights:

Tonti settled on relatively modest performance modifications for the V7 Sport engine to give it a freer-revving, more sporty character: a much "hotter" camshaft (more valve lift, duration, and overlap), higher-compression pistons (9.8:1 versus 9:1) of slightly smaller diameter (82.5 millimeters versus 83 millimeters, with matching cylinders) to bring displacement down to 748 cc (from 757 cc), larger carburetors (30 millimeters versus 29 millimeters), aluminum valve collars, and a new dual-point ignition timer and dual coils (replacing a single-point distributor and one coil).

The rest of the major engine changes—crankcases with "waffle" webbing, revised timing case to accommodate the front-mounted alternator, crankshaft modified for use with the alternator—were structural to accommodate use of the engine in the new frame and to reinforce it to handle more

power and higher revs. To complement the new engine, Tonti lightened the old Ambassador "manhole-cover" flywheel, which reduced the effects of engine torque on handling, allowed the engine to rev quicker, and reduced clunking when shifting gears. Vents from the valve covers to the breather box were also added to help purge water vapor from the top end.

By the time the prototype was finished, the frame had gained mounts for the gas tank, and accommodations for great convenience features such as the removable lower frame rails and the pivot-up seat (with convenience light underneath) and stainless rear fender. New footpegs on the Sport fold out of the way in the event of a crash or a touch-down in a corner, and the foot controls were made more sporty, with a toe-only shifter pedal (versus the heel-and-toe pedal on the V700), still on the right-hand side with one-up for low, and a slightly shorter brake pedal on the left.

Fitted to the front was a fork of all-new design, much lighter, with internal springs, innovative cartridge-type dampers, and alloy sliders. Clamped to the forks tubes are perhaps the most innovative and elegant handlebars ever fitted to any motorcycle, the adjustable swan-neck clip-ons. A slim, black-painted alloy casting on each side links the chrome-plated headlight bucket to the fork and allows room for the swan-neck clip-ons to be slid up or down on the fork tubes to accommodate rider preference. Even though the new frame was to gain fame for its stability, Tonti played it safe and fitted a hydraulic steering damper, controlled by a black plastic knob on the top triple clamp. Rear shocks were the best of the day, Konis.

For quicker steering and less unsprung weight, Tonti specified slimmer tires, 3.25x18-inch front and 3.50x18-inch rear, on stouter Borrani Cross rims. A short, slim stainless-steel front fender further cuts unsprung weight. Brakes are a twin-leading-shoe type on each side of the hub in front, and a twin-leading-shoe type with full-width shoes on the rear.

And all those parts were styled into a harmonious whole that is as good looking as any motorcycle ever designed. Key elements include a graceful gas tank, triangular locking toolboxes that nestled perfectly within the frame rails, handgrip and footpeg rubbers with matching patterns molded in, and a graceful, sweeping exhaust system with an X-shaped crossover beneath the transmission and long, racy-looking mufflers with "shark-gill" louvers cut into the rear extension. As sport oriented as the Sport is, it also has a few uncommon convenience features that make it a great street bike, including a car-type ignition switch (activates both the ignition and the starter when turned full-lock clockwise) mounted on the frame just in front of the tank that also unlocks the steering-head lock and opens the electric fuel tap on the left side of the tank. A start button was also put on the right bar for hands-on-the-bars starting.

As good as Tonti's prototype was, convincing management of the new machine's virtues turned out to be the biggest challenge of the whole project.

"Six Seconds" to Production

Before design of the new engine was finished, Tonti mounted one of the engines used in the June 1969 record trials in one of his frames and took it back to Monza to have famed Guzzi test rider and racer Luciano Gazzola wring it out. With the new frame, Gazzola was able to improve on the previous lap times, but only to what he called a "marginal" degree, because the speed bowl at Monza favors horsepower over handling prowess and cornering clearance. (On a normal road-race course, however, the new frame would make a very large difference, indeed.)

Knowing he would face an uphill struggle to get management's approval to build the Sport, Tonti made up a little "fib" that he would use, if necessary.

What in reality had been minimal improvements was exaggerated to "six seconds per lap with the same rider and engine," a figure that hinted at revolutionary changes and championships that could be won. More important, it's the kind of easily digested figure that managers can grasp and marketers can use. Of course, anybody who knows motorcycles and racing is going to know how preposterous this claim is, but it might just work on the first person he had to get on his side, Direttore Produzione Alberici, a man Tonti described as being "not so fond of motorcycles"—and presumably, not so knowledgeable, either.

In July, the production department poured over the prototype to assess it for production. After the assessment, Alberici called Tonti in for a meeting. "He pointed out that there were at least 151 changes compared to the V7," said Tonti, according to an interview he gave in the December 1997 *Ruoteclassiche*. "I pointed out to him that there were many more than that, if he was counting"—a quip that probably didn't help gain Alberici's favor.

This lightly tuned 850-cc version of the Sport was raced in the 1971 Bol d'Or 24-hour endurance race at Le Mans, France, in September 1971. The Guzzi led the race for the first 10 hours, but mechanical difficulties and a crash dropped the Sport back to third place. In honor of its excellent showing, the Guzzi 850 was nicknamed "Le Mans."
Moto Guzzi

Frames on most production Sports, beginning in 1972, were painted black. Many for the United States were painted silver, as on this unrestored 1973 example. By early 1973, U.S. V7 Sports were fitted with the flat-sided taillight shown here. Sports for the rest of the world retained the round taillight.

Tonti argued vigorously, first using the facts. He reminded Alberici of De Stefani's goal of "200 kilometers per hour, 200 kilograms, and five speeds" and that the new machine met them all. He also reminded Alberici that De Stefani wanted a serious competitor for 750-class production racing, and that these goals were not achievable without the major revisions he had designed into his V7 Sport. When the facts failed to sway Alberici, Tonti pulled out the last and longest "lever" he had: "six seconds," as in words to the effect of "Yes, Direttore Produzione, there are many changes on this machine, but it is so superior that with the same engine and rider it lapped Monza six seconds faster than the world-speed-record bikes of last year." As Tonti had hoped, Alberici knew enough to be impressed by but not enough to question the claim.

Even so, Alberici was not entirely convinced, so he postponed his decision.

Despondent and frustrated by Alberici's indecision, Tonti left the meeting and went to see Gazzola, making sure the veteran test rider would back him up on the "six-seconds" story if anyone asked. Gazzola agreed, and Tonti's little exaggeration became an unquestioned "fact" for the next several decades.

Tonti left work for the traditional August holiday, but it was a time of worry rather than rest for Guzzi's chief engineer. "They were very stubborn, so I was ready to quit," said Tonti in *Ruoteclassiche*. "I had a resignation letter ready and I was prepared to deliver it after the holidays." Fortunately, he never had to submit it. By the time Tonti returned to work, Alberici had decided to proceed with preparing the Sport for production.

In the end, Tonti's "six seconds" story had proved decisive in convincing Alberici, and it passed through the company and out into the world, eventually becoming part of Guzzi lore. Alberici latched onto it and repeated it, using it on his own bosses to justify the decision to put the V7 Sport into production. Then his bosses repeated it, and they made sure the public-relations department took maximum advantage of it. After having started such a chain reaction of repetition, Tonti is (understandably) reluctant to change his story, repeating it most recently in an interview in the December 1997 *Ruoteclassiche*.

Why stick with the story for so long? Well, for one, he was employed by Moto Guzzi until 1990 (he has also worked as a consultant more recently). And, forced to stick with it for over 20 years, he probably sees no need to ever change it. But others who were there that day at Monza have been a bit more candid. Given the fabulous result of Tonti's little exaggeration, who can deny that the end really did justify the means?

The Legend of Telaio Rosso

Elated, Tonti, Todero, and many others began the daunting task of developing the V7 Sport prototype for production, in fall of 1970. But despite Alberici's assessment of "151" parts changes, the V7 Sport was essentially an all-new motorcycle, and the process of taking it from prototype was a long process. This all proved maddening for Tonti, who was most eager to get the V7 Sport onto the streets and race tracks of the world to prove that he really had morphed the old Guzzi "buffalo" into a thoroughbred racer, so he came up with another interesting way around the company bureaucracy: hand-build a special series of V7 Sports in the racing shop to homologate the new machine for racing, and then make these special Sports available to works and privateer racers, dedicated enthusiasts, and to moto-journalists for test riding.

It was a good plan, allowing the Sport to reach the market much quicker than otherwise possible, and in a form sure to give it an instant advantage on the track and in road tests, whetting appetites for the production machines that would follow. Managing Director De Stefani saw the wisdom of the plan and readily agreed to start production in the spring of 1971.

Thus began a new Guzzi legend. The legend of *Telaio Rosso* (which means "Red Frame" in Italian), the special, hand-built V7 Sports painted in colors chosen by Tonti himself to at once connect the new machines with Guzzi's glorious racing heritage and set them apart from all that would follow—a metallic lime green for the gas tank and toolboxes to suggest the zinc-chromate green of the 1950's dustbin-faired racers and bright red for the frame to hark back to the earlier Guzzi racers.

The front brake on most Sports is a four-leading-shoe unit that actually stops very well when properly adjusted. Sport forks were built by Moto Guzzi, and are possibly the first cartridge-type forks fitted to any production motorcycle. Note the swan-neck clip-ons and the alloy headlight brackets that allow clearance to adjust the bars up, down, fore, or aft.

Everything about the *Telaio Rosso* is special, compared to the production V7 Sports. Each frame was hand-welded of thin-wall chrome-moly tubing making them the ultimate realization of the Tonti frame, stiffer, lighter, and stronger than the production mild-steel frame.

Engines were hand-assembled, "blue-printed," and balanced by the meticulous craftsmen in the experimental and racing department. Connecting rods and crankshafts were mirror polished, looking "like works of art," according to Seth Dorfler, who once owned one of the only two street-going *Telaio Rosso* officially imported into the United States. As a result, these engines are tighter, quieter, smoother, and more powerful than production engines. Crankcases have the "waffle" reinforcements of the production cases, but the castings are often rougher in appearance.

Forks were also hand-made, with 35-millimeter tubes (production tubes are 34.7 millimeters in diameter). The swan-neck clip-ons were also works of art, made from machined forgings and hand-bent tubes rather than stampings. Rear shocks were Koni's best. Said Tonti, "For this Sport, all the best parts were used to get it very fast and stable."

All the major castings save one, the rear-drive housing (the same as used on the Ambassador and V7 Special), were prototypes, often sand cast. Rear drive housings were the same polished "starburst" castings used on Ambassadors/Specials, but the internals were hand-assembled and blue-printed.

Transmissions on *Telaio Rosso* are unlike those on any other Guzzi, having their own set of internal gears, shafts, and other parts, all wrapped in a non-ribbed case (similar to the four-speed's case) designed to take the five-speed internals. The transmission was also meticulously assembled and shimmed.

Even the gas-tank decals are unique, consisting of a black banner, edged top and bottom in white, stretching from the knee recess to the front of the tank. The name "Moto Guzzi" is reversed out of the black, and a small gold eagle is embossed in the decal, just to the front of the company name.

Basically, the *Telaio Rosso* are hand-built race bikes with all the creature comforts, convenience features, and reliability of the standard Sports. As such, a mystique has built up around them that is not matched by any other Guzzi twin—perhaps because they are the only V7 Sports that truly lived up to Tonti's goals of 200 kilometers per hour, 200 kilograms, and five speeds, but also because few were built, and so these machines command prices far higher than do regular-production Sports.

Most official sources say 150 *Telaio Rosso* were built in 1971. Most of these machines were sold in

Europe, especially in Italy and Germany, but a few were sent out to Guzzi distributors in Holland, Belgium, France, Spain, Germany, Switzerland, Austria, Denmark, Australia, and South Africa. American importer Mike Berliner remembers getting two of them, and said he thought they were both sent back to Italy. It appears likely, though, that they were not. One was repainted and modified into the "MB Sport," a special show bike with shiny mylar decals, parts of which, at least, I know are still in the United States. George Kerker, racer and "road man" for the West Coast distributor, also got one, according to Ivar de Gier, who carried on a long correspondence with Kerker and was even sent a photograph of the machine. Its whereabouts are unknown.

These "civilian" bikes are the literal *Telaio Rosso* in that they have the red-painted frame, but there were many other similar machines (meaning with the chrome-moly racing frame and the hand-assembled engine, with varying degrees of the other special parts, depending on when and for what purpose they were built) constructed for works racers and for

An 850 racer built in the Guzzi racing department for an American team to campaign in the endurance race at Mosport, Canada, in 1972. The bike was doing very well in the race until present owner Al Phillips was thrown off the machine when the transmission—a production gearbox that should have been recalled—locked up. According to Torello Tacchi (another member of the team), "All of a sudden, boy, we see Al flying in the air! I'm talking maybe eight, 10 feet in the air, tumbling and the motorcycle crashing." After the crash, they got it back in the race, but it later swallowed a valve, forcing them out of the race. Tacchi also said the engine was "clapped out" when they got it, so it may have been raced in Europe before being sent to the States. Photos in a magazine article show that the machine was fitted with the small plexiglass fairing that was then optional. *Jon Tree*

factory prototype testing. Some were also built for privateer racers and for favored customers. These numbered an additional 50 or so, for a total of "just over 200 machines," according to Todero, as told to Ivar de Gier.

Despite the small number actually built and the normal attrition expected over so many years, there are probably more red-framed Sports in existence today than ever. As Dave Richardson, purveyor of wisdom and Guzzi parts at Moto International, quips, "They made 150, and there are only 500 left." So, should one get all excited when a *Telaio Rosso* comes up for sale and pay lots of extra money for it? Yes, if it's real.

The problem comes in positively identifying a particular machine as a genuine *Telaio Rosso*. True, most of the "fakes" were built because the owners liked the color combination, rather than in hopes of deceiving anyone, but one must be very careful before paying the premium these machines command because positively identifying them is a task for experts. The builders of *Telaio Rosso* were not regular production workers, so the frame and engine numbers often are more confusing than they are helpful. Some engines and frames are marked with the normal "VK" designation, followed by a series of numbers. Others have only numbers. Still others have a "C" (for *Corsa*, or racing) in addition to the "VK" or just the "C" and some numbers. The only way to be absolutely sure the machine is genuine is to write the factory, which has lists of frame and serial numbers.

Competition

The V7 Sport made its debut at the 500-km production race at Monza in July 1971 with Raimondo Riva at the controls. In a hotly contested race against twins, triples, and fours from Norton, Ducati, Triumph, Laverda, and Honda, rider Riva piloted the essentially stock *Telaio Rosso* Sport (it even had lights, speedo, and tach in place) to a respectable third place behind a Triumph Trident (first) and a Honda 750 four-cylinder (second).

With this excellent showing on the Sport's track debut, Moto Guzzi had high hopes for the future and began preparing for more races, including the Bol d'Or 24-hour race, held at Le Mans, France, on September 11–12. Moto Guzzi entered a special half-faired 850-cc version of the Sport with Vittorio Brambilla and Guido Mandracci as riders. They led the race for the first 10 hours, but mechanical difficulties and a crash dropped them back to third at the finish. In honor of its excellent showing, the 850 racer was nicknamed the "Le Mans," a name later applied to Guzzi's first 850-cc sport bike. In fall 1971, a specially modified Sport was entered in a different kind of competition, the Premio Varrone, a design competition held in the city of Varese. This machine didn't win the prize,

but it was an interesting look into the future of Moto Guzzi. Tonti's entrant was updated with an 850-cc race-kitted engine, round-slide Dell'Orto carbs with straight manifolds and velocity stacks, Lafranconi mufflers, a frame-mounted half fairing, and a slim seat with rear hump, somewhat similar to the seat later used on the 750 S. It also had triple discs, with a feature that would later be used on production Guzzis: linked brakes.

First Reviews

Tonti and Moto Guzzi were proud of the Sport and encouraged the importers to make it available for magazine tests. While not tested, the Sport was mentioned in a report in the October 1971 *Cycle World*. The first test published in the United States came two months later in the same magazine, when Carlo Perelli tested it in Italy. Prominently mentioned is the almost complete lack of promotion on the part of Moto Guzzi. Perelli attributed this "strange policy" to the fact that "requests for the new Guzzi far exceed production capacity." He also mentions the very high price, the equivalent of $2,500 (at a time when an Ambassador cost about $1,700). His opinion of it was remarkably sober: "Moto Guzzi has been successful in . . . transforming the elephantine Ambassador into a good sports model."

Others were a bit more effusive. The March 1972 *Motorcycle Mechanics* called it "a superb machine in both design and engineering." The magazine also ran it through the quarter mile in 13.2 seconds, about 1.5 seconds faster than was typical for the Ambassador. In the January 1972 *Motorcycle Illustrated*, the editors concluded that "Overall, the impression is of a fast, serious machine. So fast, in fact, that it is . . . of interest only to those who wish to compete in production machine racing."

The Sport was fitted with a small but very functional instrument cluster that included a speedometer, tachometer, and warning lights. CEV "snuff-box" switches were one of the few weak points on the whole machine.

For 1974, all markets but the United States got a new model, the 750 S. It is basically the twin-disc V7 Sport sold in the United States, but with a new seat and sidecovers, blacked-out mufflers, and racing stripes on the tank and sidecovers. *Moto Guzzi*

Famous racers even got into the act. Tonti got his friend Mike Hailwood to test a *Telaio Rosso* and recalled, "lovely Mike told me [it is] very stable and maneuverable." Hailwood also wrote up a review of the machine that was published in England. Moto Guzzi even tried to recruit Hailwood to race the Sport, but the factory could not afford to pay his usual fee.

1972 Production V7 Sports

In November 1971, regular factory production began for the V7 Sport. The basic form of these Sports is the same as for the *Telaio Rosso*, but they are factory-built machines rather than hand-built specials. The first machines received the same metallic lime green paint on toolboxes and gas tanks as on the *Telaio Rosso*, but the frames were painted black. Underneath that paint lies one of the major differences between the red- and black-frame machines: Instead of thin-wall chrome-moly tubing, thicker, heavier, less-expensive mild-steel tubing is used. Other cosmetic changes are also apparent, including "waffle" ribbing on the transmission case (to match that on the crankcase), a restyled rear-drive housing with an integral sump (some early production Sports may have left the factory with the old "starburst" rear housing, however, as explained further in the road-test section that follows), and new tank decals (without the black background and the eagle, and with red-and-white stripes above and below the company name).

Many other changes are not so apparent, however. Inside the gearbox is a new set of gears, shafts, and other internals, with slightly different overall gearing. Fork tubes are 34.7 millimeters in diameter rather than 35 millimeters, and are used with slightly revised sliders and internals. Swan-neck clip-ons are functionally the same but are made of stampings rather than machined forgings. And many of the castings are better finished, being made from production molds rather than sand castings. As the year wore on, other color combinations were

introduced, including metallic burgundy with a silver frame, green with a silver frame, and bright red with a black frame.

And a new option was added for the production machines—a spring-loaded sidestand attached to the left front engine mount. For safety reasons, spring-loaded stands are in favor nowadays, but they were a rarity in 1972. The new stand was certainly slim and light compared to most, but it was a shaky perch on which to place a new, expensive sport machine, sometimes self-retracting when the bike was parked. "Most people seem to have thought the sidestand a good deal at the $10 they added to the price of the machines—until they used them," said V7 Sport owner Glenn Bewley. "That's when Guzzi started making its money on that sidestand." Unfortunately, a similar sidestand is still used on sport Guzzis to this day.

Sports were slow in coming to the United States, and only a few of the green-and-black ones made it. Reno Leoni got one and turned it into a Formula 750 racer. Few dealers remember getting one, but Torello Tacchi, a dealer in the Chicago area, got a green one with a silver frame. In his area, the Sport was "not a very hot mover, because back then very few people liked the low bars. Eventually we just raised up the bars to help persuade people into trying them, and of course once they drove it, they loved it." Dealer Mike Harper, in the Kansas City area, had a much easier time: "When we could get them, they sold well. I was ordering and calling and screaming to get them." And his customers loved their Sports: "Better than half of them still have them. You couldn't pry them out of their hands with a jackhammer."

V7 Sports were fitted with the same transmissions as used on the Eldorados and 850 GTs. Early transmissions were recalled to be fitted with updated parts. The problem and recall are explained in chapter one.

U.S. Reviews

Results of the first real road test conducted in the United States were presented in the July 1972 *Cycle*. The machine reviewed was black with a silver frame and the starburst rear drive housing. They wrung it out on the track at Bridgehampton, revving it to 8,500 rpm (7,500 is red line) without problems. On the street, they found it to be over-geared, but able to accelerate "voraciously" when there was room enough to let it rev. The only major fault they found with it was the lack of an air cleaner. In a test in the April 1973 *Two Wheels,* the editors characterized the Sport as "a masterpiece even more rare than the fabled Agusta" and "in many ways the perfect motorcycle."

A test in the September *Motorcyclist* found the Sport's performance exhilarating, but commented more on the Sport's practicality for day-to-day use, commenting that it is "More than a motorcycle . . . a work of art."

1973 V7 Sport

For 1973, the V7 Sport was available in burgundy metallic with black frame, red with black frame, green with a black frame, and somewhat later, black with a black frame.

A number of other changes were made to U.S. models only. A larger, flat-sided CEV taillight replaced the round Lucas unit. Starting with frame number VK 14000, U.S.-model Sports were revised to have left-side footshift and right-side rear brake pedal. This change necessitated revised linkages for both brake and shifting. Shift linkages lost the Heim joints (replaced by a cheaper linkage), and the linkage from the brake pedal to the brake was changed from a cable to a rod. Later in the year, starting with engine number 33448, the timing gears were replaced by a set of sprockets and a timing chain. The oil pump was also revised to work with the new drive scheme.

At about the same time the gears gave way to sprockets, the "Moto Guzzi" decals on the tank gave way to metal badges with the company name, and Sebac shocks replaced the Konis. Decal stripes were applied above and below the badges.

Racing

Moto Guzzi continued to campaign V7 Sports in 750-cc and 850-cc forms in production, prototype, and endurance racing during 1972, including a return to Le Mans. Again, the bike was an 850, and Brambilla and Mandracci were the riders. This time, they led the race for the first 18 hours, but in the end took fourth.

In 1973, Guzzi entered a very special works racer in the Barcelona 24-hour race at Montjuic, with Raimondo Riva and Luciano Gazzola at the controls. This racer was fitted with triple Lockheed disc brakes and a very highly tuned 850-cc race engine. Despite a hard-fought race and many difficulties, Gazzola and Riva brought the Guzzi in fifth. This machine more than any other, including the 1971 Le Mans racer and the Premio Varrone bike

The Eldorado and 850 GT were replaced partway through 1974 by the 850-T, a new model that was halfway between the V7 Sport and the Eldorado. At first, the model was named the Interceptor (and small "Interceptor" decals were fitted to the sidecovers), but the name was quickly dropped. The pipes on this machine, with the constant-radius bend and fixed to the heads with the old screw-in clamps, may have been fitted to some very early production Ts, but most were fitted with pipes having a different bend and two studs on each head to affix each pipe. Note also the shiny mylar trim, which quickly peeled off most machines when they were put in use.
Dave and Sharon Hewitt

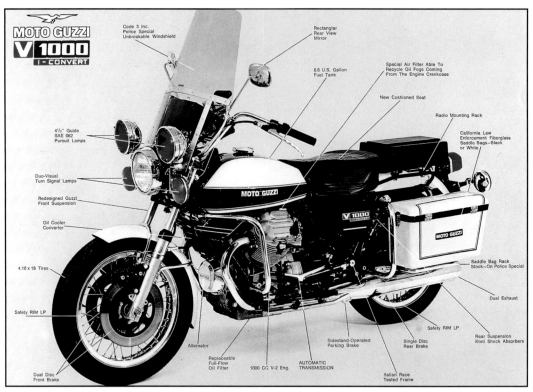

The very first batch of production Converts sent to the United States arrived in fall of 1974 and were sent to the LAPD for use by their drill team. One was even road-tested for the December 1974 issue of *Hot Rod* magazine. The Convert was most likely the first production Guzzi built with many of the features commonly thought to have been introduced on the 850-T or T3, such as an oil filter, larger Bosch alternator, linked brakes, and "four-fin" valve covers (some very early Converts, including the one tested by *Hot Rod*, have the old-style covers). Most early U.S. market Converts were in the police configuration shown here. Note the flat-sided taillight like that first used on U.S. V7 Sports. Later Converts had a unique tailpiece and light. Note also the spoilers on the front crashbars, which were designed in the Guzzi wind tunnel to keep the front tire firmly planted, to prevent the speed wobbles that afflicted some earlier police Guzzis. *Dave and Sharon Hewitt collection*

of the same year, is the true predecessor to the production 850 Le Mans.

1974 V7 Sport

For 1974, the V7 Sport was only offered in North America. Other markets received the similar 750 S. Some early 1974 Sports have four-leading-shoe front brakes, but part-way through the production run, dual-disc front brakes became standard. These disc brakes were some of the best of the era, and were certainly a great improvement over the old four-leading-shoe front brake. Most, if not all, 1974 Sports were painted black on black and were fitted with the metal tank badges and square-sided CEV taillamp.

750 S

Instead of the updated V7 Sport with twin discs and left-side shift that was imported to the United States in 1974, other markets got the 750 S, which was essentially the same motorcycle with a few cosmetic changes that gave it even more of the

cafe-racer look. Some believe that this is the best-looking Guzzi ever. Except for the "four or five for very special customers," Mike Berliner did not import the model to the United States.

The most striking change was to the paint scheme. Gas tank and toolboxes are black overall but the black is overlaid by racing stripes on the tank and sidecovers. Stripes were available in red, orange, or green. To add even more street-racer menace to the look, the shark-gill mufflers were painted flat black and the seat foam was cut away to make it thinner while a hump was added at the back. Some of these seats were fitted with a thin chrome trim piece tracing the lower edge of the seat on each side, while others were not.

Like the 850-T that went on sale a little later that year, the 750 S was fitted with new-style lockable toolboxes that extend farther to the front than do the Sport's triangular toolboxes. The S was fitted with the round taillight used on European and early U.S. Sports, left-side shift, Aprilia turn signals, and 17/21 primary reduction gearing in the transmission.

850-T

The first real fruit of the De Tomaso regime, the 850-T, initially called the Interceptor (at least in the United States), made its debut at the Milan exposition in late 1973. "Moto Guzzi engineers have taken the best technical features of the touring models . . . and combined them with the frame and suspension of the fantastic V7 Sport to create the new 850-T," boasted the sales brochure. Functionally, the new machine was better in every way than the Eldorado it was designed to replace. Styling was another matter, at least for American customers.

It began entering dealer showrooms about midyear, available in salmon red, metallic bronze, metallic green, and black, all with metal tank badges, metal "850-T" badges and "Interceptor" (in the United States) decals on the toolboxes, and gaudy gold mylar tape stripes (which often began to peel off in the first month of use) on the tank and toolboxes. It was certainly modern looking, but in a bland and generic way, part Kawasaki 900 and part Benelli. Its looks and performance gave the 850-T broad appeal in most of the world but quickly ruined U.S. sales momentum for the marque. For reasons unknown, the Interceptor name was dropped soon after the first machines reached America.

Guzzi's new touring machine owed much more in style and function to the V7 Sport than to the Eldorado, resulting in a sleeker, lighter, more versatile machine, less suited to American-style touring but with much better handling. Its frame was based on the excellent frame Lino Tonti had created for the Sport. Onto this frame, Tonti and his staff had fitted a really well-padded touring seat, a 25-liter gas tank, fairly large stainless-steel fenders, and twin toolboxes with lockable sidecovers (similar to those used on the 750 S).

The 850-T engine is a mix of V7 Sport and Eldorado. Like the Sport engine, the T engine carries an alternator up front under a polished aluminum cover, a dual-point timer with dual coils, 30-millimeter carbs and "filter-free" rubber plenum, and a tachometer drive off the front of the camshaft. Crankshaft, cylinders, cylinder heads (except for the method of fastening the exhaust header pipes to the heads), and pistons are more similar to those on the Eldorado. The Premier brochure for the 850-T claimed an output of 65 horsepower from the new engine, with a 9.5:1 compression ratio.

Cylinders on the 850-T were made to accommodate future increases in displacement by moving the pushrod tunnels farther away from the centerline of the chrome-plated bore; this basic casting would be used through the end of the round-head Guzzi line in the early 1980s. Similarly, the cylinder-head castings were revised to accommodate the new spacing for the pushrod tunnels and for an important update—two studs instead of an internally

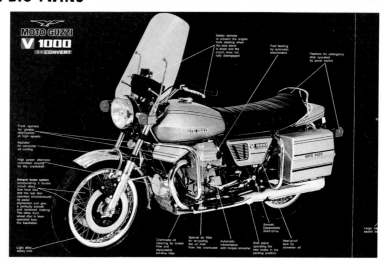

threaded port to retain the exhaust header pipes—but were otherwise unchanged, retaining the same chamber size and shape and valve sizes first used on the Ambassador. New rockers and a new head gasket were also used with these heads to accommodate the new pushrod spacing.

Perhaps the most enduring of the 850-T's parts would be its new cam, which went on to power even the high-performance Le Mans models, through the square-head Mark III, and even some California models into the early 1990s.

New header pipes, crossover, and mufflers made their debut on the 850-T, and they would serve as the "base" exhaust for many of the new round-head Guzzi models to come. Instead of the smooth 180-degree curve of the earlier Guzzi pipes, these new pipes bend sharply, straighten out briefly, and then bend back sharply to the horizontal section that goes into the crossover. The mufflers are large chrome megaphones with a seam top and bottom and a dimple on top to allow removal of the rear axle.

One carryover from the Sport that shouldn't have been is the weak, 14-amp Bosch alternator. It is just adequate to power the starter, ignition, and basic lights on the machine when it is new and operating properly and is hooked to a good battery. Fortunately, this alternator and all its regulator and rectifier were updated during the 850-T production run to a 20-amp Bosch system that proved much more suitable to a full-boat touring machine. The 20-amp system would be used on all following Guzzi big twins through the mid-1980s.

Compensating somewhat for the weak alternator, Guzzi fitted a beefy new Bosch starter that soon gained an excellent reputation for power and reliability. This starter's solenoid sits atop the main body, rather than being underslung, as on the Eldorado. It was used on all the following big twins until the late 1980s.

Civilian-spec Converts began arriving to dealers later in 1975 with the tailpiece and taillight shown. *Bob Farris collection*

A beautifully preserved example of an 850-T3 police model, with siren, radio, flashing lights, and all.

Though the T was clearly an offshoot of the V7 Sport, the hand controls were clearly not. The 850-T got normal handlebars and "modern" switches, with the wires routed inside the handlebars. This routing gives a cleaner look, but complicates changing handlebars.

More of the generic styling is evident in the headlight and its mounts, which are an extreme retrograde step from the distinctive pieces on the Sport. On early machines, the headlight shell was chrome plated, but on later ones it was painted black; all used a chrome-plated ring, however. American models came with a sealed-beam bulb requiring a different housing than the one on world-version models, which used a replaceable bulb and separate reflector. Aprilia turn signals and the flat-sided taillight were carried over from the U.S. Sport. Instruments on the T are a basic speedo and tach in a similar mount (with four warning lights) to the one used on the Sport.

The forks fitted to the 850-T are similar to those fitted to the disc-brake V7 Sport and 750 S, except that the tubes are spaced wider (195 millimeters versus 180 millimeters). The single-disc Brembo system used on the T is basically the same used on the disc-brake Eldorados—a 300-millimeter cast-iron rotor and Brembo F08 caliper—but it seems to be slightly more effective, probably because the T weighs less. The factory also offered a kit to add a second disc.

In hopes of taming wear to the splines used throughout the Guzzi driveline, a cush drive was added to the T rear wheel. Because of the space

taken up by the cush drive, the brake hub could only be half as wide as before, so Guzzi designed a narrower drum and shoes for the 850-T rear brake and made it a double-leading-shoe design to compensate for the drum area. Like the V7 Sport's twin-leading-shoe rear brake, the T's is way too grabby (*Two Wheels* magazine called it "a mite overefficient" in January 1975).

Two updates were made to the five-speed transmission used on the T: the pair of gears for fifth were made larger and stronger, while keeping the overall ratio the same, by switching to 21/28 teeth rather than 18/24. Late in the year, the bronze thrust washers at the front of the mainshaft were replaced by a caged needle bearing.

Sales

In Europe, the T sold to expectations, but in the States it didn't sell well at first. It came out about mid-1974, when some dealers still had V7 Sports and Eldorados on the floor. If you were touring oriented, which would you likely have picked? How about if you were sport oriented? As a result, sales of the T got off to a slow start. "I think they alienated a lot of people when they switched over to a sport-type bike," opined Seattle dealer Bob Budschat. "BMW did the same thing in the early '70s when they went to sport-type bikes. We got a lot of those Beemer boys onto Guzzis because we still had the Eldorado."

Clutch-Plate Problems

During the time the T was in production, Guzzi got what seemed to be intermittent batches of bad clutch plates. "On the very first of the Ts, and most everybody got some, the rivets were soft in the clutch plates and the hub would break loose from the plate," remembered Dave Hewitt. Some of these bad plates made it into the parts pipeline, so simply substituting new plates was no guarantee of a fix. Savvy dealers devised their own fix: "Ken Johnson and I fixed a bunch of them by heli-arcing the hub to the plate," continued Hewitt.

According to John Gregory, a Guzzi distributor who frequently visited Italy and Moto Guzzi during this period, the factory that made the plates "was about to go on strike, so the workers didn't put the rivets in right. We had problems with those for years after. It got so bad that Guzzi would give out the drawings to whoever would build a batch of plates."

Second Year

For 1975, the 850-T was carried over essentially unchanged, but later in the year, an important but unannounced change was made: a cartridge-type oil filter was added (more on this in the next section).

In the United States, the T was the only model available for much of that year, and even it wasn't available consistently. Once the T was the only option, sales began to pick up. "The T sold OK, but it sold on inertia," said sales rep Dave Hewitt. "There was a crop of customers that had been thinking about an Eldorado for a year or two. It was mainly first-time Guzzi buyers that were in the flight pattern to buy a Moto Guzzi who made it sell as well as it did."

Some U.S. dealers did really well with the Ts, however. What did it take to get them to sell? Ken Johnson, Mike Harper, and others resorted to dolling-up their 850-Ts to look like Eldorados. "We took our bikes and put the great big California Eldorado fender on the front," said Johnson. "DB here in Tulsa took a mold off the Eldorado rear fender, and we put that cap right over the stainless-steel fender that was on there to give it an Eldorado look in the rear. Then we'd paint the whole bike—bags and accessories and all—like an Eldorado. You can't believe all the colors we used off of the muscle cars of the day—Green Go and Grabber Orange and all different colors." Other dealers simply gave up and stopped selling Guzzis.

V1000 I-Convert

The V1000 I-Convert, so named for its semi-automatic transmission with a hydro-kinetic (*idro* in Italian, hence the "I") torque converter, was actually the first of the 1975 models out the factory gates (albeit in very limited numbers initially), and was thus the first to actually debut features normally attributed to the 850-T3 or S3, namely triple discs with integrated braking, an oil filter, and the new airbox with filter. So to give the Convert (the Rodney Dangerfield of Moto Guzzis?) the respect it is due, these features are discussed in this section.

The first examples of this new model reached the United States in the early fall of 1974 for delivery to the LAPD drill team (and in time to be road-tested for the December 1974 *Hot Rod* magazine). The first ones available for civilian purchase were also police models, which were painted black and white, had a solo seat, a trapezoidal-shaped master cylinder (some had the round master cylinder), Harley-style sidestand, and the flat-sided taillight from the T. Later civilian machines were painted black (with gold or white striping), silver, or ice blue (the latter two with black striping), and most of these had a new tailpiece, taillight, and round master cylinder.

The Convert story began in 1970. According to Wally Maxwell, former LAPD officer and salesman for police accounts for ZDS Motors, his boss, Bob Blair, and Mike Berliner had heard reports of a new Honda with an automatic transmission that was then being built for testing with Japanese police forces. Since they were working so hard to sell more and more Guzzis to U.S. police, they decided to ask that Guzzi begin work on an automatic. About the same time, Moto Guzzi also began considering the

A factory brochure for the California version of the 850-T3. Californias differed from standard T3s in having high, braced bars, black-and-white buddy seat, footboards, and hard bags. *Seth Dorfler collection*

design of an automatic transmission for the Servizio Scorta (Italian escort police), according to Lino Tonti, who began adapting the automatic transmission for motorcycle use, assisted by Todero.

The first machines to be tested outside the company were based on the 850 GT. A brief piece in the October 1973 *Motorcyclist* magazine describes the machine and mentions that several were sent to the United States, where they were tested by the LAPD and the CHP. None of the officers interviewed for this book remember much about these tests, but a few recall seeing the machines. Nevertheless, the tests must have proved encouraging, because Moto Guzzi kept developing the concept, and when the production machines came out just over a year later, the LAPD was the first customer.

The torque converter Tonti chose was built by the German company Fichtel and Sachs. It was mounted to a pressed-steel flywheel, which was mounted in place of the normal flywheel and clutch. To give better acceleration for in-town use and better economy for highway use, the converter was linked through a small multiplate clutch to a unique two-speed transmission to give both high (22/22) and low ranges (18/24), changed by a heel-and-toe rocker pedal on the left side. Low range can take the Convert up to about 80 miles per hour. High range can easily be used in town, as well, because the engine will pull from a standstill to its 100-mile-per-hour (approximate) top speed, just a little more sluggishly at first than if low range were used. Use of the clutch is necessary only when shifting the transmission between high and low ranges.

The 750-S3, released in 1975, was the last of the Guzzi 750s that were based on the big-twin engine. It was a combination of features from a number of different models: the linked brakes, swingarm, rear drive housing, and forks first used on the Convert, an 850-T engine with smaller 82.5-mm bores and pistons, the same basic tank that had been used on the V7 Sport and 750 S, and nonlockable sidecovers also used on the 850-T3.

The converter is about 90 percent efficient, with 10 percent of engine power lost to heat, so a pump and an oil cooler were fitted to circulate the fluid and shed this heat.

To compensate for the losses in the torque converter, Tonti did what many automotive engineers did before him when faced with the same problem: increase engine displacement. He increased the bore to 88 millimeters while keeping the same stroke to give the Convert engine a displacement of 949 cc. Iron liners were fitted to the cylinders.

Integrated Brakes

The Convert introduced what would become a hallmark of the marque: triple disc brakes with the patented Moto Guzzi linked braking system. As fitted to the Convert, this system used a 12-millimeter master cylinder and hand lever on the handlebar to operate the right front caliper and a 15-millimeter master cylinder inside the right sidecover to operate the rear caliper and the left front caliper off the foot pedal.

Tonti had been developing linked brakes since the 1950s. He had used a mechanical linkage on the Dama, an ill-fated super-scooter that he designed in the early 1950s. When he came to work for Guzzi in 1967, he began experimenting with another mechanical system on a V700, but the mechanical linkages were too complex to be very effective. Later, he began developing a new system using hydraulics, and it showed real promise. Todero took over development of the system, and did a lot of work with Brembo to balance front and rear braking so that the rear brakes would lock first under all conditions. Todero wanted to release a system that operated all the brakes off of the front hand lever, but the system was unacceptable for use on German-market machines because that country's inspection agency, the TUV, required separate controls for the front and rear brakes.

Todero's compromise was to switch to the system already described.

Contrary to popular myths, this system does not automatically compensate for load or even proportion more braking force to the front discs (although many later Moto Guzzi models were fitted with a proportioning valve). On the first Converts, a simple manifold splits the fluid from the master cylinder equally to the front and rear calipers.

The main advantages to this system are that the rider's foot controls about 75 percent of the braking power (freeing the right hand for throttle control and steering the motorcycle) and it reduces the tendency for the chassis to pitch forward under hard braking. On his racing Guzzis, Dr. John Wittner used this latter characteristic of integrated braking to control chassis attitude on the entry into corners, but he also used it because when operated properly, it stops the motorcycle really quickly and safely, with less drama.

Air and Oil Filters

As previously mentioned, some late 850-Ts were fitted with an oil filter, but the system was first commonly used on the Convert, and the earliest Converts may have actually gotten the feature before the T. The filter is a small car-type cartridge filter that threads onto a boss and fitting in the oil pan. In some ways, the system was really innovative and had advantages over an outside-filter system— oil passages are shorter and the filter is out of sight and out of harm's way—but it also required removal of 18 screws to get at for service, creating another one of those *perceived* problems that has cost Guzzi many sales. "For years, customers complained there was no oil filter," said dealer Jim Tagaris. "Now the customers pissed and moaned because they had to take off the sump to change the filter, so we didn't gain a thing." Even in 1998, this problem persists.

Moto Guzzi also (wisely) fitted the Convert with an air-filter system, the first *effective* one on any Guzzi and the first at all since the demise of the Eldorado. It consisted of a tubular paper element in a snorkel-like airbox extending forward between the cylinders and rubber manifolds to route filtered air to each carburetor.

Many other small changes were instituted on the Convert engine, including a new timer with a revised advance curve and 31 degrees of automatic advance, a new flywheel with static-advance mark at two degrees and full advance at 33 degrees, a cable system to actuate the cold-start circuits in the carburetors (the 850-T had individual levers on each carb), the uprated alternator fitted to the late 850-Ts, restyled valve covers (these have four "fins" on top and taper in depth toward the outboard edge; some very early Converts, including the one featured in *Hot Rod,* have the T-style covers) with

The fluorescent orange panels on the 850 Le Mans were billed by Guzzi as a safety feature. This is a highly modified 1977 version.

A 1976 Le Mans brochure shows the taillight and seat that were used only for that year. Molded of a rather delicate self-skinning foam (no covering was used), these seats quickly broke apart in use. For 1977, a new seat was used, made of a slightly different foam and with more seating area for a passenger. For 1976, the Le Mans was available in red or gray-blue. For 1977, white was added as an option. *Dave and Sharon Hewitt collection*

vent lines attached by banjo fittings, and revised pushrods and tappets.

Rear Drive and Swingarm

A new-style drive housing made its debut on the Convert. Overall, the new housing is 2 millimeters longer, so the right fork of the swingarm was shortened to compensate. This housing would be used on most Guzzis to follow for the next 20 years, but inside it and the driveshaft tunnel in the swingarm were many parts unique to the Convert, including the gearing (3.778:1 versus 4.714:1) and a unique U-joint with integral driveshaft.

Other Features

Front and rear crashbars, floorboards, hard saddlebags (with removable tops), and a tinted windscreen were standard. The Convert was designed from the start to carry a windshield. To prevent the high-speed wobbles experienced on the earlier shield-equipped American police machines, the Convert was fitted with a steering damper and a wind-tunnel-designed spoiler on each side of the front crashbar to exert downforce on the front end.

Safety and car-like convenience were two of the main themes for the Convert. With the key turned on, the electric fuel tap on the left starts supplying gas to the carbs (the right petcock is mechanical and acts as a reserve). To start the "Guzzi-matic," the rider has to have both hands on the bars, the left to pull in the clutch (a cut-out is integral with the clutch cable) and the right to push the start button. The long, Harley-type sidestand also must be stowed, or a switch cuts out the ignition. When the sidestand is deployed, a cable-operated caliper clamps onto the rear disc to prevent the bike from rolling away if parked on a grade.

A tachometer wasn't really needed because of the automatic transmission, so a new instrument housing was fitted, which had a speedometer in the center, flanked by warning lights, a small knob to reset the trip odometer, and switches for courtesy lights and emergency flashers.

Reviews

Perhaps fitting for such a car-like motorcycle, the Convert was road-tested for *Hot Rod* magazine's December 1974 issue. Tester Bob Greene wrote up a hyperbolic review, calling it "the newest and most innovative thing in motorcycling" and (even he must have been snickering a bit) a "sexy dude" that "handles like the proverbial cat." But he wasn't through yet; reaching for the stars, he added, "At last someone has closed the gap between touring bike and racer."

While the Convert is no racer in stock form, it is a comfortable, decent handling machine, and with a little engine work, can be made into a very nice undercover hot-rod.

The Convert found a ready market in some countries—it was popular for sidecar duties—and was a total sales flop in others. In many areas of the United States, it was a top seller, making up somewhat for the loss of the Eldorado. Some dealers, like Mike Harper, "could never get enough" to meet demand. One Seattle dealer "ordered them 20 at a time" according to sales rep Bob Budschat. Others didn't even order any because they "knew" their customers would never accept it. Nevertheless, the Convert was a steady seller for many years in the United States. "It wasn't our best seller," said Dave Hewitt, "but it had a niche—people who had a physical disability or were elderly or towed a trailer. And it made a really nice machine for the passenger on the back because they weren't getting jerked around with each shift."

The LAPD Drill Team

The first batch of 30 Converts went directly to the LAPD in the fall of 1974, according to Dick Studdard, captain of the drill team:

We bought 28 for the drill team and a couple of others for the sergeants because we had so many Harleys breaking down on our grass drills [maneuvers held on grass fields in stadiums and parade grounds] that it got embarrassing. I had sent out memos recommending that we put pressure on Harley-Davidson to supply machines that were more reliable or to find something else for the drill team. Nothing happened until one day when we performed for an academy graduation and Chief Ed Davis got to see our performance. It was embarrassing. We had about eight Harleys break down during the 12-minute grass drill. After the drill, the chief walked by me and said, "You made your point."

When they got the new machines, which team mechanic Frank Ortiz calls "slip-and-slides," Ortiz set about modifying them for team use: "First, we eliminated the linked brake by plugging the line from the rear master cylinder to the front disc because otherwise you'd have drill-team members falling all over the street." Then Ortiz rigged up special wheel lights on the spokes, to add flash to the machines.

According to Ortiz, Studdard, and other former drill-team members, the Converts were perfect for drill work. The slow, precise maneuvering was hard on the clutches of normal machines, but the Guzzis took it all in stride. They kept their beloved "slip-and-slides" until 1977, when they switched to Kawasakis.

Other police forces, all over the world, bought the Convert. A common complaint was that the batteries would discharge because the torque converter kept the engine at low rpm. Dealer Torello Tacchi solved the problem by fitting the larger Nippon-Denso alternator off of the Suzuki GT 750 "Water Buffalo," which was a copy of the Bosch, right down to the taper on the rotor. He had to re-drill the three mounting holes for the larger diameter of the N-D case and make a spacer for the alternator cover, but once installed, "That thing would start to charge at idle," he said.

Problems

Some of the early Converts had problems, but they were the kind of problems that showed up many miles down the road for most riders, faster under the severe use of regular police duty. The first problem was that the stamped flywheel-torque-converter assembly would crack. At first, these were replaced under warranty, but with identical parts that often failed in the same way. For 1978 (according to a June 1978 Premier service bulletin), a new, heavier, machined flywheel was put into production and the problem was cured. Also that year (according to the same bulletin), the ATF pump's inner rotor was redesigned to allow a longer engagement area with the driveshaft to prevent stripping of the hex engagement surface. As a note, proper attention to fluid level in the converter system is critical. Too little, and the torque converter will burn out; too much, and seals will blow.

Other Updates

After the first batch of Converts was built, a few changes were made, most notably to a different taillight with an odd-looking tailpiece. Beginning in 1978, a plastic vented alternator cover and weird, plastic lockable gas cap began being fitted. In 1979, cast wheels, a new taillight, new switches, a proper recessed gas cap with lockable metal cover,

A new seat and taillight were introduced on the Le Mans for 1977. The taillight was later used on several other models, including the 1000 SP.

The 850 Le Mans even made a decent drag racer. Willy Gregory won several NHRA nationals and set records in the E Modified Sportster class, beating Japanese four-cylinders in the process. The engine was fitted with Ferrari rod bearings, lightened flywheel, stronger valve springs, 1,000-cc barrels sleeved down to reduce displacement under the class limit of 946 cc, and Venolia pistons, among other modifications. Weight was shaved down to the class limit of 550 pounds for bike and rider by changing the front end and taking off all nonessential gear. *Seth Dorfler collection*

and a new throttle were introduced. During 1980, starting on engine 215000, the iron-lined cylinders were replaced by Nigusil-plated ones. (Nigusil is Guzzi's proprietary nickel-silicon plating process developed for some of its racers in the 1950s and first used on the production big twins starting with the 850-T4 in 1980.) Convert production may have continued as late as 1984 for police customers, but civilian production stopped in 1982.

850-T3

In mid-1975, Moto Guzzi released a remarkably improved version of its 850 that at last realized the promise in the basic design. The most visible update—triple disc brakes—was reflected in the "3" in "850-T3." It was available in the standard version for all markets, a California version (with higher bars with bracing, footboards, windshield, saddlebag, police sidestand, black paint, and another version of the black-and-white Harley-type seat with special chrome hand rail) that was mostly sold in European markets, the T3FB version (with the higher bars and footboards, but with the normal seat) that was mostly sold in the United States and Canada, and a police version (with a speedometer only, higher handlebars, white-painted fenders, solo saddle, and a longer sidestand). Other subvariants that were essentially different combinations of the features listed above were also offered in some markets. Standard colors included brown, black, green, maroon, silver, and ice blue. Though introduced in 1975, the 850-T3 wasn't consistently available in many markets until the late fall of that year or even the early spring of 1976. Also, the California and FB versions were not immediately available in all markets. The FB, for example, wasn't available until at least late 1976 in the United States.

The 850-T3 motor received all the updates to the basic Guzzi engine first introduced on the Convert, including crankcases and sump (for the oil filter), ignition timer, carbs, valve covers, and air filter.

The T3 chassis was mostly based on the Convert's, as well: same basic frame, swingarm, suspension,

brakes, wheels, lights, tank, sidecovers, and rear drive housing (but with 4.714:1 gearing instead of 3.778:1). Some changes are hidden inside these parts, however. The gas tank lacks the fuel-level sensor of the Convert tank and the U-joint and driveshaft on the early T3s are like those on the Ts. Later T3s have a larger U-joint and carrier bearing.

Many other small changes were instituted on the T3, including a new housing for the speedometer and tachometer, a cutout switch in the clutch cable to prevent starting until the clutch is disengaged, non-lockable sidecovers with plastic louvers at the front and "850-T3" badges (also, "California" badges on California models, "FB" transfers on footboard models), and nonfolding pegs on standard (non-footboard) models.

With all these changes, the 850-T3 was truly a world-class touring machine. Its styling still wasn't as suited to the American market as the old Eldorado's had been, but it was so functionally excellent that it was once again winning new customers for Moto Guzzi, in all markets.

By 1977, the standard U.S. model was the T3FB. At the end of 1978, the 850-T3 was discontinued for the United States, but stock remained to be sold off in the following year. In 1979, the factory made many changes: new taillight, cast wheels, seat, longer-travel fork dampers, and hand controls like those on the 1000 SP, and a lockable gas-cap cover, CEV headlamp and turn signals, and vented plastic alternator cover. In 1980, the 850-T3 was replaced in most markets by the new 850-T4, but some civilian T3s may have been built as late as 1982.

The T3 sold well, but didn't recapture the glory days in the United States. "The 850-T3 was more accepted than the T because people were starting to say, 'Well, if I can't get an Eldorado I might as well look at this,' " said Mike Harper. Also, dealers like Ken Johnson and Harper who dressed them up sold plenty, and most U.S. dealers cite the footboard models as much better sellers than the regular T3. "I think the floorboards helped a bit," remembered Harper, "but you have two schools of riders: those who wouldn't have floorboards on their bike and those that wouldn't have pegs." For Europeans, the 850-T3 was an attractive model, especially the Californias. On both sides of the Atlantic, though, it's common to see 20-plus-year-old T3s still in service as daily rides, and that is the best testament to the real appeal of the T3.

750-S3

The last of the 750-cc Moto Guzzis based on the big-twin engine (several later 750s were built up from the small-twin engine) was the 750-S3, introduced early in 1975 but not widely available until later that year. It was also in the line-up for part of 1976. Although it may look like the 750 S of the prior year, it was a much-changed machine, with an 850-T-based engine (pushrod tunnels farther out from the bore centerline, milder cam, header pipes affixed to studs on the heads) and a chassis (swingarm, linked brakes, rear drive housing) and electrics (larger capacity alternator) based on new components first introduced on the Convert, rather than those used on the V7 Sport. Unfortunately, like its predecessor, this model was not imported into the United States.

The basic structure of the S3 engine is the same as that of the 850-T engine except for the bore, which is 82.5 millimeters, rather than 83 millimeters, requiring different cylinders, pistons, and rings. The exhaust pipes are unique to the 750-S3, having the smooth curve of the V7 Sport header pipes but with the two-stud mount to fix them to the cylinder head. Later S3s were fitted with the ignition timer of the Convert (with revised advance curve).

The S3's gas tank was basically the same as that of the V7 Sport, but the hinge on the cap was moved to the rear end of the assembly. The new sidecovers are not lockable. Unfortunately, the swan-neck clip-ons were replaced on the new model by conventional clip-ons, and the S3 was a bit slower than the Sport or S because the S3 was fitted with the milder camshaft first used on the 850-T.

850 Le Mans

When most people think Moto Guzzi, they think Le Mans, and with good reason. This model, more than any other, gave Guzzi a high profile in the world of sporting bikes. In fact, it was a profile all out of proportion to its actual performance, which was barely higher than the early V7 Sport of five years previous. Never mind all that because the Le Mans had going for it what by then was even more important than actual performance—the *look* of performance—and this gave it the edge to win the most important race of all, the race out the showroom door. The Le Mans was built for the 1976–1978 model years, initially in red, then in ice blue, and still later in white.

It all began even before the V7 Sport had hit dealers' showrooms with a bike built by Tonti for the Premio Varrone, an annual design contest held in the city of Varese (see the V7 Sport section for details). Tonti continued developing his show bike, on the track and off, until the new model was introduced, in fall 1975.

Styling

Cafe styling was the rage in the mid-1970s. Even Harley-Davidson got into the act in 1977, with its XLCR. Moto Guzzi produced the pinnacle of the form with the Le Mans. Its styling melded the graceful S3-styled tank with the obligatory bikini fairing and new, more racer-esque side panels and fenders, which were made of plastic. The small

The very first Le Mans in the United States was turned over to Reno Leoni, who just had time to prep the machine for Mike Baldwin to ride at Daytona in 1976. The team of Baldwin and Leoni never won the U.S. Superbike championship, but they came very close in both 1976 and 1977, and they had some notable victories, trumpeted here on this flier from Premier Motor Corporation, the U.S. importer. *Seth Dorfler collection*

fairing truly is in the "bikini" idiom, serving more as streamlining for the headlight than as a wind deflector for the rider. American models were fitted with a sealed-beam headlight, the substitution of which required adding a short snout to the front of the fairing. Adding even more flash was a day-glo orange panel at the front of the fairing.

Except for that small splash of orange and a few parts that were silver or chromed, what wasn't red (on red-painted bikes) on the Le Mans was matte black—frame, top and bottom panels on the tank, exhaust pipes and mufflers, turn-signal bodies, headlight ring, hand and foot controls, and so on. This contrast of bright and shiny with dark and flat was arresting when new on the showroom. Unfortunately, the flat black didn't stand up to the weather.

Cast wheels further added to the performance look. Spokes on these wheels are in pairs that bend in toward one another and then away again, suggesting the shape of an hourglass. They are painted silver. Bolted to the front wheel are twin discs, drilled to shed water and add to the racer styling. At the rear is a 242-millimeter disc, also drilled. These cast-iron discs gave excellent braking action, but further added to the unkempt look after a rain.

The seat was an odd one, molded of a rubbery self-skinning foam and very angular in styling. It wrapped around the rear of the tank, had a short flat section for the rider, and then a flat-topped hump at the back for the passenger. Though an interesting experiment, the self-skinning foam faded and dried out quickly in the sun, cracking and breaking apart shortly thereafter. Worse yet, even for the brief time it held together, it wasn't very

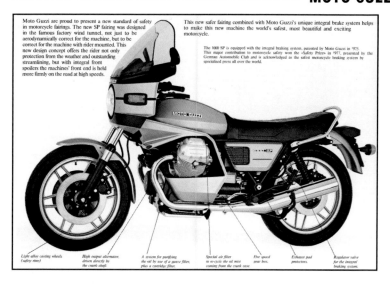

Moto Guzzi are proud to present a new standard of safety in motorcycle fairings. The new SP fairing was designed in the famous factory wind tunnel, not just to be aerodynamically correct for the machine, but to be correct for the machine with rider mounted. This new design concept offers the rider not only protection from the weather and outstanding streamlining, but with integral front spoilers the machines' front end is held more firmly on the road at high speeds.

This new safer fairing combined with Moto Guzzi's unique integral brake system helps to make this new machine the world's safest, most beautiful and exciting motorcycle.

The 1000 SP is equipped with the integral braking system, patented by Moto Guzzi in 1975. This major contribution to motorcycle safety won the «Safety Prize» in 1977, presented by the German Automobile Club and is acknowledged as the safest motorcycle braking system by specialised press all over the world.

Light alloy casting wheels (safety rims). | High output alternator, driven directly by the crank-shaft. | A system for purifying the oil by use of a gauze filter, plus a cartridge filter. | Special air filter to re-cycle the oil mist coming from the crank case. | Five speed gear box. | Exhaust pad protectors. | Regulator valve for the integral braking system.

The 1000 SP was introduced for 1978 and featured a three-piece fairing designed in the Guzzi wind tunnel. The airfoils built into the front of the fairing lowers apply downforce on the front wheel for more stable handling. Note the straight-spoke cast wheels, satin-black frame, and the big plastic tank cap. Dave and Sharon Hewitt collection

comfortable and felt awful under the rider when it was wet. Most broke up and were replaced in their first year of use.

Engine

Tonti got the extra power for the Le Mans by making the engine breathe better than the standard 850, the T3. Compared to the 850-T3 heads, the Le Mans heads have larger combustion chambers and larger valves. Hooked up to the intakes of these new heads are 36-millimeter Dell'Orto carbs, 6 millimeters larger than the square-slides on the T series, and with real diaphragm-type accelerator pumps and velocity stacks. No air filters were fitted. These carbs have side-pull arms that actuate the slide through a bell crank at the top of each carb. The crank multiplies the throw of the arm, allowing a short-throw throttle to open the slides fully, but at the cost of an even stiffer twistgrip action than on previous Guzzis. Hooked up to the other end of the heads is an all-new exhaust system with a balance pipe looping down underneath the alternator cover and upswept mufflers to keep them from touching down in turns. The entire exhaust was painted flat black, in keeping with the styling of the rest of the machine.

To take advantage of the better breathing, Tonti bumped up the compression ratio to 10.2:1. This was accomplished through use of new pistons with high domes. While these domes definitely helped performance through the increase in compression, they also make for a long and complex path for the spark on the outboard side of the head to reach up and over the dome to the compressed fuel-air mixture on the other side. The result is that these engines are very prone to pinging and run very hot, even when used with high-octane fuel.

Le Mans cylinders were fitted with steel liners rather than chrome-plated bores and new pistons

and rings to match. For the Le Mans, the steel-lined cylinders were chosen because they allow for cheaper and easier overhauling than for chrome-lined cylinders, an important consideration because the bike ran without air filters. Also, only three rings were fitted to the Le Mans pistons instead of the four used on 850-T3 pistons. To complement the new high-compression pistons and combustion chambers, the ignition timer from the V7 Sport was used rather than that from the T3 or Convert.

Changes

For 1977, the Le Mans was given several upgrades. The seat was reshaped with a shorter hump at the rear and was fitted with a strap behind the rider position that serves as a grab strap for the passenger and a hold-down strap for the seat. Though still made of self-skinning foam, the foam on this seat was less prone to cracking than that of the 1976 seat. The rear fender was redesigned for mounting the new oblong taillight with integral mount (later used on the 1000 SP and other models), which replaced the old T-style separate rear taillight and tube-shaped mounting boss built into the fender. For 1977, white became a color option. No notable changes were made for 1978.

Reviews

When *Cycle* magazine tested the Le Mans for the August 1977 issue, the editors passed it off somewhat disparagingly as a "flash bike," finding much to fault in the switchgear, seat, sidestand position, and a few other things—all fair criticisms. Even so, they found much to like, especially the handling, calling it "the only shaft-drive that handles exceptionally well when ridden hard." The editors stated further that "It ranks among the top five handlers in the street/sporting world, chain or shaft . . ." but eventually they caught on to its true character, concluding that "Compared to most flash-bikes, the Le Mans' great strength is its versatility. It has the integrity for the twisties, the smoothness for the Interstate, and the suppleness for around-town putting and puttering."

Racing

Though its design was a bit dated in the era of the four-cylinder, the Le Mans did well in endurance and AMA Superbike events. Racing kits were even offered, with a hotter camshaft, straight-cut close-ratio gears for the transmission, different primary-reduction ratios, 40-millimeter Dell'Orto carbs and manifolds, 40-millimeter open-megaphone exhaust, and eventually, after it had been developed by Reno Leoni and shown to his friend Lino Tonti, a sump spacer to cut down on power loss from "windage" in the crankcase.

In the United States, the most successful Le Mans Superbike team was the Premier-sponsored effort pairing Reno Leoni as tuner and Mike Baldwin as rider. To help launch the new model, Mike Berliner gave Leoni the first Le Mans imported, just in time for Leoni to prep the machine for its debut at Daytona, in the spring of 1976. Unfortunately, Leoni didn't have time to fit wider rims and racing slicks, so Baldwin finished out of the winner's circle. Even so, Leoni was hopeful for the future: "We had some advantages because the rules said you had to use the standard frame, and the Guzzi frame was much better than the Japanese frames."

By the start of the season's second race, at Loudon, New Hampshire, Leoni had made many modifications to the machine, among them wider rims. Baldwin out-rode everybody that day to take the surprise victory.

A while later, they were back at Loudon for a club race to try out a new modification. According to Baldwin:

We knew we needed to fit a wider tire to be competitive. In order to do that, we needed to cut the swingarm away a little more, which meant machining the driveshaft down about a quarter inch. We were testing that out at the club race, and the wider tire worked great.

[Gary] Fisher and [Reg] Pridmore [on BMWs] were at that race, and they were the guys we had to beat. I was arguing with Reno about whether or not that shaft was going to last. Anyway, I got the holeshot and was leading the race. About a lap from the end, the driveshaft broke. Before the next race, we made a new shaft out of special steel.

For the rest of the year, Leoni kept developing the engine:

I made a lot of changes. Mr. Norris and myself came up with two beautiful camshafts. All my Le Mans were short strokes with 92-millimeter bore, making it almost 1,000 cc. We changed the cam bearings to ball bearings. I also used a ball bearing on the front of the crankshaft but kept the plain bearing on the rear because of my experience with the 750 racer. On the front of the crankshaft, it was very easy to put in the ball bearing. We stayed with the stock plain bearings for the rods.

On August 22, Kurt Liebmann rode Leoni's Guzzi in the Superbike national at Pocono, Pennsylvania. Liebmann normally rode a Berliner-sponsored Ducati, but on this day, he rode the Le Mans to victory over the 1,000-cc Laverda and 750-cc Ducati that took second and third. Guzzis triumphed again at Pocono in October, Baldwin taking first and Liebmann second in the 200-mile endurance race.

In 1977, Baldwin and Leoni went at it again, finishing consistently, despite some bad luck and crashes. Baldwin remembered one in particular:

At Loudon in 1977, I was leading the race, when I crashed on the last lap and slid up almost to the start-finish line. The bike was laying on top of me. Reno ran across the track and picked the bike off of me. He started to push it, but I said, "No, no. If you push it, I'll get disqualified." I pushed it the last 10 feet to cross the finish line, but the AMA docked me a lap for having outside assistance. That put me back in sixth for the race. In reality, nobody had pushed me across the line, but the California boys [the Butler and Smith BMW team] had protested.

Proving that the Loudon win the previous year wasn't a fluke, the Guzzis of Baldwin and Liebmann took first and second at the Charlotte Superbike event, both beating Wes Cooley on a Yoshimura-prepared Kawasaki. To Baldwin, such finishes aren't surprising at all; what is still surprising and frustrating is that they didn't win the championship: "The Guzzi was as fast as anything we were running against. We did well at Riverside and at Sears Point. If it weren't for the crash on the last lap at Loudon, I would have won the Superbike championship that year."

For 1978, Baldwin raced both the Guzzi and a Ducati, losing the Superbike championship by the margin of another disqualification. He also raced a TZ750 to the U.S. Formula 1 championship and signed with Kawasaki for the following year.

In the spring of 1979, Leoni took the Le Mans back to Daytona for the last time. Freddie Spencer was scheduled to ride the Guzzi and Jimmy Adamo was to ride a Leoni-prepared Ducati. During preliminaries, Spencer was clocked at 159 miles per hour on the Guzzi, according to Leoni. Unfortunately, Adamo crashed a 250 Yamaha that he was also racing there, so Spencer was given the Ducati to ride.

Le Mans 850s were campaigned by many other teams in local and national sprint and endurance races, in many countries. At first, it was competitive, but with each passing year, Moto Guzzi allowed its Le Mans to be left farther behind in Superbike competition. Eventually, the rise of twins-class and endurance competition rendered the Moto Guzzi competitive again.

In 1980, the SP was revised to make it more comfortable by adding a thicker seat, lower footpegs, and wider-spaced lowers for more knee room. In some markets, this machine was called the SP NT (for New Type). Other changes included mufflers with less rise (the mufflers on this bike are aftermarket), gloss black paint on the frame, and less black paint on the bodywork.

1000 SP

Since 1950, Moto Guzzi had had in its backyard a little-used asset that most manufacturers would have killed for: a wind tunnel. While it had been used to great effect in developing the incredible dustbin fairings used on the Guzzi racers of the 1950s, its effects were hard to see on any of the production bikes—until Guzzi unveiled a new touring mount at the Milan show in late 1977 for the 1978 model year. That model was the 1000 SP, Moto Guzzi's first fully faired production motorcycle. The new model was available in white, gold, silver, a very light green, and ice blue (and maybe a few other colors for specific markets). The first version of the SP was built for 1978, 1979, and part of 1980.

The most visible difference between the SP and other Guzzi big twins is the innovative three-piece fairing designed by Lino Tonti, with help of the wind tunnel. Over a period of six months of after-hours testing (the electric wind-tunnel fan

Two red-and-white schemes were offered on the SP— the one shown, and a reverse of the pattern.

draws so much current that it can only be used after production shuts down for the evening), the fairing was refined to offer excellent protection from wind and rain and to streamline and stabilize the motorcycle. This fairing consists of a fork-mounted upper fairing and two-piece lowers that mount to the frame. The lowers wrap around behind and below the cylinders to provide very good weather protection for the rider's legs, but they were also cleverly designed with cut-outs that expose almost the entire cylinder to the airstream. The left lower limited access to the oil dipstick, so an extension tube and longer dipstick were fitted.

Because they wrap around behind the cylinders, intruding on rider knee room, the lowers force an even more rearward rider position than Guzzis already had, so two concessions were made to deal with the associated problems. First, spoilers were designed (with help of the wind tunnel) into the front of the fairing lowers to apply downforce on the front wheel. Second, to take advantage of the increased load on the rear wheel caused by the new riding position and to "balance the braking power," according to Lino Tonti, a larger caliper was fitted to the rear brake (Brembo F09) than to the front (Brembo F08), along with a true proportioning valve in the integrated braking system (the first Guzzi model to use one).

The proportioning valve is a sophisticated device that allows three separate ratios of front/rear braking force, each triggered at a different threshold of system pressure. With the addition of a proportioning valve, the integrated braking system reached a new level of sophistication, allowing rear-wheel-only braking in delicate situations, slightly rear biased braking under normal stops, and strongly front biased braking under hard use.

Befitting its role as a touring machine, the 1000 SP was given more than the usual complement of instruments, all clustered together in a molded rubber dash behind the fairing. Instruments include a speedometer with tripmeter, tachometer, quartz clock, voltmeter, ignition switch, and full complement of warning lights. Hand and foot controls are from the Le Mans, although the handlebar switches were improved, and the throttle downgraded from a quality metal Tomaselli unit to a plastic one. Like other 1978 models, the tank was fitted with a large plastic gas cap.

Front suspension is an updated version of the standard Guzzi fork, with longer dampers (with 1 inch more travel) and caliper hangers behind the fork sliders; also, the sliders are painted black, except for a band of polished aluminum at the top. Fenders are similar in style to those used on the Le Mans, only longer. In keeping with the times, cast wheels were fitted, some early ones with straight spoke pairs, and later ones with "hourglass" spokes like those fitted to the Le Mans.

MOTO GUZZI G5

Premier Motor Corp.
Hasbrouck Heights, N.J. 07604, Tel: 201/288-9696

The 949-cc SP engine was basically a Convert engine with the 850-T camshaft, the slightly different crankshaft for use with the manual transmission and clutch, and the standard front timing-case cover. With 100 extra cc over the standard 850 models, the SP had quite a bit more torque than the smaller models. To gain cornering clearance on its new sport tourer, Moto Guzzi fitted it with an upswept exhaust, similar to that used on the Le Mans, but the exhaust was chrome-plated. To go with the upswept mufflers, a longer deployment arm was added to the centerstand, which brought the side benefit of providing useful leverage to hoist the bike onto the stand.

With its larger engine and new fairing, the SP is an excellent sport tourer, with enough power and wind protection to cruise all day at 80–100 miles per hour, and the optional removable hard bags make it even more practical as a tourer. Weak points of the package include its thinly padded seat, easily damaged switchgear, poor-quality original paint, and curious use of a lot of matte black paint on the frame and footpeg mounts, tank top, parts of the fairing, and on many other parts. As on the Le Mans, this finish suffered the same fate after the first rainstorm or the first few weeks under a hot sun. Nevertheless, the 1000 SP was a good seller around the world in its first years.

The SP remained in production essentially unchanged for 1979. Thankfully, Guzzi did make one update, to a revised gas tank with a recessed gas cap and lockable metal cover. Late in the year, however, the 1000 SP front and rear suspension received a few updates, according to a *Circolare Technica* dated November 1979: the double fork seals in each leg were replaced by one double-lip seal, and the rear shocks received updated rubber blocks on upper and lower mounts.

A groovy 1970's dude poses with his 1978 G5 on this Premier brochure. The G5 was essentially a Convert with a five-speed in place of the automatic. Starting in 1979, the G5 was fitted with cast wheels and a metal gas cap with a lockable metal cover, replacing the plastic unit shown. *Seth Dorfler collection*

The Le Mans II was something of a cross between an 850 Le Mans and a 1000 SP. From the Le Mans came the engine and brakes. Just about everything else was from the SP or was new to this model. *Moto Guzzi*

In 1980, many changes were instituted to make the SP a better, more comfortable touring machine: Nigusil-plated cylinders (beginning with engine number 215000), new mufflers with almost no upsweep, the lower and farther forward footpegs from the T3, revised front turn signals, the thicker seat from the Convert, wider spacing of the lowers for added weather protection and more knee room, softer kneepads, revised forks with silver sliders (they had been black), and the almost complete elimination of matte-black paint on the bodywork. Functionally, the new machine, called the SP "NT" in some markets, is much improved, being more comfortable and easier to keep clean. Visually, the NT looks more sedate, definitely more of a tourer and less of a sport machine.

Despite the improvements, the SP was becoming overshadowed by the many new fully faired touring mounts that began to enter the market, and sales began to plummet. The next update to the SP came in 1982 with the introduction of Dell'Orto PHF 30-millimeter carbs with rubber manifolds for U.S. models, and two new paint jobs, in red on white and white on red. On one, the center panel on the fairing is red, while on the other the same section is white. Same goes for all panels on the machine. In these bright new colors (and in ice blue), the SP was back again for 1983 and part of 1984, before being replaced by the SP II.

By 1983, the SP was failing badly, most noticeably in the United States. The U.S. market had become flooded with unsold Japanese bikes offered at ridiculously low prices. Of equal weight, Premier Motor Corporation was forced to give up its shrinking but still profitable import business by Alessandro De Tomaso, who wanted to consolidate sales of Moto Guzzis with sales of Maserati automobiles at Maserati North America. Thus began the era of "car guys" handling (or mishandling, depending on whom you ask) Moto Guzzi in the United States, and the SPs that stacked up in the warehouses during the rough transition were eventually sold for a reduced price in later years, both to unload stocks, and because the new importer paid Mike Berliner "25 cents on the dollar" for Premier's stock of motorcycles and parts.

G5

The other new model for 1978 was perhaps a natural follow-on to the Convert. Some police departments and civilians wanted a basic machine with the larger engine of the Convert and the five-speed transmission of the T3. Guzzi gave it to them in the form of the G5, which stayed in production through about 1982 in civilian trim and in police form until 1985. Standard equipment varied in different markets, but in most of them, front and rear crashbars, hard saddlebags, and a windscreen were included. American police bikes were in black and white. Civilian machines were painted various colors for different markets, including salmon red, ice blue, silver, and black.

Police models have taller handlebars, a Harley-type sidestand, and footboards, while the civilian bikes were fitted with footpegs, a small tachometer tacked on at the back of the instrument console, a dog-legged sidestand, and a centerstand with an absurdly long deployment arm on the left side. The footpegs on the civilian G5 were mounted to the same brackets used for the footboards, so they were lower and farther forward than on the 850-T3.

Early G5s were fitted with the plastic alternator cover, SP-type switchgear, lockable plastic gas cap, and the following parts off the Convert: taillight, tailpiece, crashbars, front spoilers, seat, and Borrani rims. In 1979, the machine was revised along with most of the other bikes in the line-up by fitting a revised gas tank with a recessed gas cap with a lockable metal cover, CEV headlight, and the following parts from the 1000 SP: cast wheels, seat, and taillight. Later in the year, front and rear suspension were upgraded with a single double-lip seal in each fork slider and revised rubber for the rear shock mounts. In 1980, Nigusil-plated cylinders began to be fitted (beginning with engine number 215000). In 1982, the G5 was updated with Dell'Orto PHF carburetors and rubber manifolds.

The G5 looks, feels, and acts like a torquier 850-T3, except that it is even more comfortable, footboards or not. *Motorcyclist* tested the G5 alongside the Benelli *Sei,* Ducati Darmah SD, and Laverda 500 Zeta. Not surprisingly, the Guzzi wasn't the first choice on twisty roads, but when faced with a 500-mile ride home after the test, according to the report, "Everyone wants the Guzzi." For civilians and police alike, it made a good utility bike, excelling at nothing, but pretty competent for just about any use. "They sold well," too, according to former dealer John Schwartz, "especially if you decked them out to look like a police bike."

Le Mans II

The Le Mans II is basically a cross between an 850 Le Mans and a 1000 SP and was released in late 1978, for the 1979 model year. From the Le Mans came the engine, matte frame, seat, "hourglass" cast wheels with drilled rotors, side panels (but with "Le Mans II" badges), and exhaust. From the SP came most of the rest—fairing lowers, wider front forks, molded rubber dash, and so on—with a new upper fairing thrown in to give it its own unique character. This "mix-and-match" Le Mans was available in red, white, and royal blue, and was offered for the 1979, 1980, and (part of) 1981 model years. The Le Mans II was not imported to the United States.

The new upper fairing is similar in style to that of the SP, but it is much smaller, has a rectangular headlight and shorter windscreen, and lacks the mirrors that are standard on the SP fairing. It is also less rounded, and its rectangular headlight and painted panels on the whole machine seem to eliminate completely any curving lines. As pointed out

by CX 100 owner Nolan Woodbury, the wind-tunnel-designed spoilers built into the fairing lowers improve stability and gave a more "planted" feel to the front end.

Changes

In late 1979, the Le Mans II suspension got the same upgrades as the SP and G5 suspension (fork seals and shock grommets). In addition, from frame number 19718, new fork dampers were fitted, and the spacer between the fork-spring pair in each leg was installed inverted to prevent the springs from cocking it such that it seizes on the damper rod.

For 1980, fairing lowers were given new mounts that space them out slightly farther from the centerline to allow more knee room, and Nigusil-plated cylinders (with updated pistons) replace the steel-lined cylinders and matching pistons, starting with engine number 80390. Later that year, beginning with frame number 22636, air-adjustable damper cartridges for the front fork and air-adjustable rear shocks were fitted. No changes were made for 1981, and the model was replaced during the year with the Le Mans III.

CX 100

The Le Mans II had an American cousin, and like most things modified to suit American tastes, it was bigger but not as fast. Bigger, that is, in displacement only, having the same 1,000-cc engine

Instead of the Le Mans II, U.S. dealers got the CX 100, which was basically the same as the Le Mans II, except that the 949-cc engine from the SP was substituted for the 850 engine. Why? Mike Berliner says it was because American dealers demanded a larger engine. Unfortunately, the larger engine didn't bring with it more performance. The fairing on the CX 100 and Le Mans II was also designed in the Guzzi wind tunnel and features much more angular styling and better wind protection than that of the 850 Le Mans.

and 30-millimeter square-slide carbs with an air filter and airbox as the SP engine. Except for the sealed-beam headlight and 80-miles per hour speedometer required by American regulations, the smaller battery of the 850 Le Mans, and the "CX 100" badges on the side panels, the rest of the package was just like that of the Le Mans II. The CX 100 was offered in red or in metallic ice blue for model years 1979–1982.

Why the change of engine for the United States, especially when the Le Mans powerplant is more powerful? Most sources say that the 850 Le Mans engine could no longer pass U.S. emissions regulations. That may or may not be true, but it is not the reason the CX 100 got the 949-cc engine from the SP. Here's why, according to Mike Berliner:

Let me explain it this way: every time we brought in a machine, at every dealer's meeting, they always said, "Can you make it a little bigger? Can you give it more power?" In America, they always wanted bigger and more power.

That bike was built because the Americans wanted a larger capacity machine. If it was less powerful than the 850, it was because the factory didn't take the time to make it more powerful.

With the advent of the 949-cc engine from the SP, Guzzi suddenly had a way to give Berliner and his customers a bigger motor in a Le Mans package.

Thus came to pass something of an orphan model, but a good one nonetheless. And, in truth, most riders really didn't miss the extra power as much as they thought they would. Although the CX 100 engine lacked the "edgy" power of the Le Mans engine, it had more torque and about the same power in the lower rpm range that is used most by most riders. According to figures in the July 1980 issue of *Cycle* magazine, the CX 100 ran the quarter mile in 13.50 seconds at 98.46 miles per hour, which is about a half a second and 5 miles per hour slower than the 850 Le Mans they had tested for the August 1977 issue.

For actual use on the street, the CX 100 is far more practical than a "real" Le Mans because it has a real air filter and a low-stress engine that is torquey and fast enough for most riders. If it's not fast enough, easy modifications can add a lot of extra horsepower.

Changes

The CX 100 chassis was updated in the same ways as that of the Le Mans II, and its engine in the same ways as the 1000 SP. Refer to those sections for explanation of changes.

850-T4

The last new-model Guzzi to use the "round-head" engine was the 850-T4, introduced in 1980 as the new "basic" Moto Guzzi. It was another mix-and-match model, in this case, a blend of 850-T3 and 1000 SP. The basic approach was to take an SP and strip off the lowers, replace the engine with a slightly updated version of the venerable Guzzi 850 engine (with Nigusil-plated cylinders and pistons with tighter tolerances to match), repaint the body-

work red with gold pinstripes, and add "850-T4" badges—depending on your outlook a slightly "sport-tourier" T3 or a slightly stripped, smaller-displacement SP.

The 850-T4 may be the most attractive and practical of the whole T series, having an effective top fairing, the latest switchgear, and the Nigusil-plated cylinders. Unfortunately, this model was never imported into the States. Civilian production ended in 1983, but it was built until 1985 for police use.

The 850-T4 would be the last Guzzi based on the "round-head" engine. Fortunately, the round-head was a good base on which to build the engines that would power Moto Guzzi into its future.

The 850-T4 was introduced in late 1979 for the 1980 model year. It was the first Guzzi big twin to be released with Nigusil-plated cylinders, which are a great improvement over the chrome-lined cylinders used on many earlier twins. It is a very practical and good-looking street bike, featuring the SP fairing without the lowers. This model wasn't imported into the United States.

CHAPTER 3

THE TONTI-FRAME SQUARE-HEAD GUZZIS
Le Mans III through California EV

By the early 1980s, the old Guzzi round-head engine, and indeed the styling on all the big twins, was looking as dated as their performance. For several years, the bulk of Alessandro De Tomaso's attention had been focused on a new line of small twins that he had Lino Tonti develop, hoping to double Moto Guzzi's output. De Tomaso had even opened a second production facility in the Innocenti car works that were also part of his empire.

At first, the small twins were conventional in style, looking much like miniature 850-T3s, but before long, two new bikes made their debut that showed the rising influence of De Tomaso and his Modena styling bureau. These were the V35 Imola and V50 Monza, with small plastic fairings and tailpieces integrated with the seat. Soon after, the new "Modena style" was carried over to the Le Mans line, with more plastic and an angular new shape to the engine. Not long afterward, all the big twins were remade in the new image.

Le Mans III

For 1981, a new Le Mans was released that was radically restyled and civilized compared to the Le Mans II and CX 100. Restyled like the Monza and Imola, with a similar theme for the bikini fairing, gas tank, and integrated seat and tail section in the rear, along with a new two-piece spoiler section designed to apply downforce on the front end at speed. Civilized with a real airbox and filter and a (supposedly) quieter exhaust that allowed it to pass the latest U.S. and European noise and emissions regulations. It is a good-looking machine, more sporting in style than the Le Mans II or CX 100, with better performance and a more civilized demeanor, which gave it broad sales appeal. It was available in red, white, and silver for 1981–1984. In the United States, the Le Mans III was cataloged for 1983 and 1984.

The "Square-Head" Engine

In an attempt to make the Guzzi engine appear more modern, it was given a restyle for the Le Mans III. Externally, the only difference is more angular styling on the cylinders, heads, and rocker covers. For the purposes of this book, we'll call this new engine the "square-head" engine, but the term "new" is used advisedly. There was nothing really new about it but the styling, which was instigated by De Tomaso and penned in Modena. Modern it did look (at least as modern as an air-cooled pushrod V-twin could look), and over time it proved a good engine, largely because it was based on the "round-head" Moto Guzzi V-twin Carcano and Todero had first sketched out in 1963.

The square-head Le Mans III motor was fundamentally the same as the previous 850 Le Mans

The third iteration of the Le Mans was released in 1981. It featured all-new styling and a squared-off shape to the engine top end. Tonti, Todero, and others worked very hard at designing new intake and exhaust systems that actually increased power output compared to earlier Le Mans engines while allowing it to meet the most stringent noise and pollution laws in the world. *Moto Guzzi*

This "Marlboro-pack" paint scheme was a regular color option in Europe, but it was only used in the United States on the 1987 Le Mans SE. The SE featured a black-painted engine and drivetrain and a close-ratio transmission. *Michael Dregni* motors, having the same bore-and-stroke; valve, piston, and chamber dimensions; 36-millimeter Dell'Orto round-slide carbs; camshaft; and the "high-performance" version of the ignition timer (first used on the V7 Sport). Cylinder studs were moved farther from the bore to allow for future bore increases. Spec sheets list that the compression ratio was reduced from 10.2:1 to 9.8:1 on the Le Mans III engine, but it is something of a mystery how this

was done, since bore, stroke, and chamber and piston dimensions are virtually identical. Claimed power output increased, from 71 to 76 horsepower, largely because of the redesigned intake and exhaust ports and the new airbox and exhaust.

The Le Mans III engine also was fitted with some new parts, including rocker supports made of the same alloy as the cylinder heads (to expand at the same rate as the heads and keep valve lash more

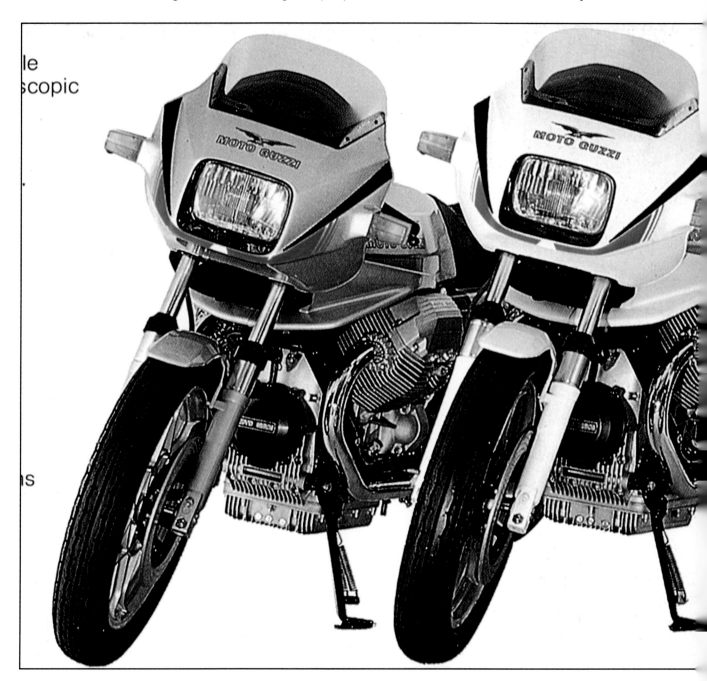

consistent, for reduced noise), Nigusil cylinders (although some late Le Mans II engines had them), and the aluminum sump spacer that was part of the late version of the 850 Le Mans and Le Mans II race kits. The sump spacer and alloy supports were carried over onto all later square-heads.

A new engine breather system uses the main backbone tube of the frame as the breather chamber. The outlet to atmosphere first goes to the new plastic snorkel-type airbox (with a rectangular paper filter) to reduce emissions. Oil return from the breather is through a rubber line from the rear frame cross tube to the oil return tube on the crankcase.

Other Changes

Although the bulk of the changes were cosmetic, a few were functional and had real impact. Umberto Todero spent a lot of time developing the

The Le Mans III was imported into the United States for 1983 and 1984. Magazines praised the return of the "real" Le Mans to the U.S. markets, and it was a popular machine, then and now. These three colors were offered. *Seth Dorfler collection*

The California II was released in the fall of 1981, with fat-fendered styling to appeal to the legion of riders who still liked the look of the Eldorado and 850 GT. It was a successful model around the world, and a version was even offered with an automatic transmission. *Dave and Sharon Hewitt collection*

airbox and exhaust so that even though the new Le Mans gained power, it was also quieter and cleaner burning. To cut noise, Todero used double-wall header pipes and mufflers, without the traditional Le Mans crossover at the front of the engine. Instead, a separate tubular crossover section fits between the header pipes and the new mufflers, which are much larger than previous mufflers. Another change: no more flat-black exhaust; these are chrome plated, adding to the modern look.

The instrument console was updated to a new molded rubber piece that placed the large white-faced tachometer front and center, flanked by indicators for the turn signals. The blue-faced speedometer is to the right of the tach and a voltmeter to the left. Centered below is the ignition switch and a row of warning lights.

Forks are air-adjustable (and have a balance tube) with new triple clamps that space the 35-millimeter tubes at 180 millimeters, the same spacing used on the original 850 Le Mans, and narrower than those used on the Le Mans II and CX 100. Fork sliders are painted the same color as the rest of the motorcycle. Rear shock absorbers are by Paoli and are also air-adjustable. A 20-millimeter longer swingarm (with a longer driveshaft inside) results in a longer wheelbase.

American models have different headlights than those for the rest of the world, and German models have a true proportioning valve in the integrated braking system (a simple manifold is used for the rest of the world), along with a larger (Brembo F09) rear caliper.

Reviews

The Le Mans III was a model of obvious appeal and sold well globally. The model didn't reach the United States until 1983, by which time the difficult transition was on between outgoing importer Premier and new importer Maserati North America. Dealers were uncertain about the new importer, and many who had weathered the increasingly tough times with Moto Guzzi through the late 1970s and early 1980s simply closed shop or switched to other brands. Thus, all the 1983 U.S. models got off to a slow start because they were hard to find. As things settled down later in the

year, the new importer began recruiting new dealers to replace the old, and shipments of the Le Mans III and other models got more consistent.

And the model was finally reviewed in U.S. magazines. "Italy's swoopiest thunderbike is alive and better than ever," trumpeted *Cycle* in September 1983. They also commented that the new Le Mans was almost $1,000 cheaper than the CX 100 ($4,518 versus $5,498). *Cycle* liked the new Le Mans, commenting that "Our test Le Mans runs quicker, quieter, and cleaner than former types." Their test resulted in a quarter-mile time of 12.66 seconds at 106.38 miles per hour, which is over 0.4 second and three miles per hour faster than the 850 Le Mans *Cycle* tested in 1977. Uncharacteristically for an American magazine, *Cycle* even liked the linked brakes, but really disliked the seat, calling it "typically full-sport Italian: board hard." With that comment fresh in mind, you can perhaps truly appreciate the accomplishment of English iron man Steve Attwood, who piloted a basically stock 1983 Le Mans III to victory in the mother of all street endurance rides, the Iron Butt Rally, in 1993. Attwood covered an astonishing 12,458 miles in 11 days.

Dr. John, 1984

With the return of the "real" Le Mans to the United States, someone was bound to take it to the track. Most notable among the many who did was a team of dedicated amateurs headed by a Pennsylvania dentist, Dr. John Wittner. Before a stint in the military and then college and dental school, Wittner had been a racer and service manager for a Guzzi dealership.

With his dental practice well established, Wittner got the itch to go racing again, and he thought the new Le Mans was the perfect machine with which to compete in the new AMA endurance-racing series. "Nobody at the time was doing any racing with them," he said, "so I went down there and made a pitch to George Garbutt at Maserati. I said I wanted to go endurance racing. I told them I would pay for the motorcycle at their imported cost, and they accepted it on the moment. I went home with an 850 Le Mans III, a fabulous motorcycle." Under the rules, the 850 Le Mans qualified to compete in the middleweight division, against the four-cylinder bikes of 750-cc and under.

While he was lining up the machine, he began recruiting friends and patients to put on a serious race effort. Among them were Ed Davidson and Kathleen Childress to handle P.R. and fundraising, Bob Griffiths as crew chief, Shirley Smrz as timer, and Nick Phillips and Greg Smrz to ride the bike (Wittner also rode, at first). Here's how former Formula 1 racer Smrz was recruited, while in the dentist's chair:

He was my dentist and asked me while he was working on me if I would like to go endurance racing.

I said, "Noooh." He said, "Yeah! It'll be fun." I told him, "You can't race for fun; you race to win."

He said, "Forget it; let's just go have fun and do this endurance race. We're not going to win." But to me, you always go to win. A bunch of my friends were involved in it. So I thought, what the hell; I'll just go for the one weekend.

The first endurance race of the season was at Rockingham, North Carolina. "The other teams laughed at us when we showed up with that Guzzi," said Smrz. "They said, 'Come on. An 850 Le Mans racing against VFR 1000s?' "

By the end of the race, no one was laughing at Team Moto Guzzi North America (the "Dr. John" moniker wasn't then used). "Turned out that that Guzzi handled so well, we won our class hands-down against some much-faster bikes," said Smrz.

"Roger Edmondson was managing that program at the time," said Wittner. "When he presented the awards he said, 'First place to the team that surprised no one more than themselves.' That was absolutely the truth. I was flabbergasted."

As impressive as it was for a start, the team just got better as the season wore on. The bike largely stayed stock, though. According to Wittner:

The bike was totally stock except for some changes to the muffler. I wanted it to look like a stock Moto Guzzi and it did. There were no tricks in there except good preparation. That bike would do four 6-hour races before we had to take it apart and look at anything. It was unbelievably reliable, a testament to good original design.

Even with a solid crew and a solid machine, it sometimes took exceptional effort on the part of the riders to win. The race at Summit Point is an example:

You should have seen Greg at Summit Point, a race that ran from late in the afternoon until just before dark. I didn't realize that the course was going to consume brake pads so heavily. When it started to get dark, he came around and we saw fire coming off the front brakes, sparks like you couldn't believe. When he came in for his last pit stop, we said, "Greg, there's something wrong with the brakes." He said, "There's nothing wrong with the brakes; there *aren't* any brakes. They went away about 10 laps ago." He rode the last half hour of that race with no brakes whatsoever, and he won.

Said Smrz of the brake-less ride: "All I can say is, that engine had a lot of back pressure!"

By the end of the season, Team Moto Guzzi and their Le Mans won the middleweight title and were reportedly denied the overall championship by a few points as a result of a "for the good of the sport" decision. The secret to their success? According to Wittner, "The idea was that the motorcycle

should never break and that the riders should never crash the bike, and if they did we would strangle them to death. The riders never crashed, and the bike never broke. Never."

After winning the championship, Wittner sold his stake in the dental practice to his partners: "I made an exit and started doing this full-time, with no income whatsoever. Things felt good and I just wanted to keep winning." And win he would.

California II

The second of Guzzi's new square-head models was introduced in the fall of 1981, the California II. This model was styled to appeal to the legion of *Guzzisti* who liked the fat-fendered look of the old Eldorado/GT and to cash in on the growing craze for custom cruisers. Standard equipment included a plexiglass shield, high handlebars, front and rear crashguards, a black-and-white seat with chrome grab rail, a chrome luggage rack, and detachable plastic saddlebags. The result was an all-around motorcycle, comfortable enough for the open road, practical enough for commuting, and stylish enough for profiling. It was available in burgundy, white, black, or anthracite.

In general style, the California II is similar to the 850-T3 California, but there were actually many differences, including a widened and stretched swingarm and driveshaft, new gas tank and side panels, chromed Eldorado-style fenders with painted center section, 10-spoke cast wheels and fatter tires (120/90 H18 front and rear), ignition cutout switch on the sidestand, SP-style exhaust (with throatier-sounding mufflers), and Paoli air-adjustable rear shocks.

The California II sported a new, 949-cc version of the square-head engine. Except for the angular shape of the top end, this engine is basically

In late 1985, the California II was revised for greater rider and passenger comfort. The buddy seat was made longer, the rear of the footpegs was lowered, and the larger luggage rack was fitted with a tail trunk (for most markets). *Moto Guzzi*

The 850-T5 fairing and instrument console are almost car-like.

The 850-T5 was introduced for 1983 as the new entry-level Guzzi big twin. It was fitted with 16-inch wheels front and rear and featured new, integrated styling by Giulio Moselli.

the 949-cc round-head engine as used on the 1000 SP and the G5. This engine will be referred to as the "small-valve." Besides the California II, this engine went on to power the SP II and early versions of the Mille GT and California III.

All U.S. and Swiss California IIs were fitted with 30-millimeter round-slide PHF carbs and rubber mountings; California IIs for the rest of the world have VHB carbs and metal manifolds until engine number VH 19637, at which point PHF carbs and rubber mounts were fitted. American models also have a different headlight and turn signals than other versions. California IIs for the German market have a proportioning valve for the integrated brakes and a larger (F09) rear caliper.

The seat was one of the few weak points in the whole California II package—too big for one, not quite big enough for two, and not as comfortable as it looks. In late 1985, starting on frame number VT17500, a new longer seat was introduced, along with revised footboards (lowered at the rear for a more natural foot position), a new grab rail at the rear, and a larger luggage rack, and a tail trunk (at least on U.S. variants). The new seat was also lockable. Some 1987 California IIs were fitted with the Saprisa alternator.

The California II was built from 1981 to 1987 and was a good seller, especially in Europe. The California II sold best where touring riders predominate. For a while, at least, the California Polizia model was also offered, as shown in a November 1985 sales brochure.

California II Automatic

In response to persistent requests from U.S. sales rep Dave Hewitt for a new version of the Convert, Moto Guzzi introduced the California II

Automatic to the U.S. market (possibly to some European markets, as well) in late 1984. As expected, the new machine was a California II chassis and engine top end mated to the drivetrain of the Convert. They were made in black or white. While Hewitt and his dealers were happy to have the automatic again, it was a bittersweet reprise: "We got it, and the stupid oil pumps—every one—twisted off like they had in the beginning. Why did they do that again?" The real problem, discovered by Dave Richardson, is that the female coupling between the ATF pump and its hexagonal driveshaft is not hardened.

Sales of the California II Automatic were good at first because of pent-up demand from Convert riders who wanted to trade up. But because of the pump problem and a bad magazine review cited by several dealers that called the California II Automatic "the world's most boring motorcycle," sales soon dropped off, and the automatic was discontinued in 1986.

850-T5

A new basic-model big twin, the 850-T5, was introduced for 1983 with an 848-cc version of the small-valve, square-head engine. Styling on this machine was the product of designer Giulio Moselli and De Tomaso's styling bureau. It incorporated the then-fashionable 16-inch wheels front and rear. It was originally offered only in smoky quartz metallic with red and yellow accents, but later it was offered in red.

Styling on the new machine was an attempt to integrate all the components into a homogeneous whole. A small, squarish front fairing covers the rectangular headlamp and encloses the instruments, but it lacks a windshield of any kind. Lines from the fairing flow into those of the new gas tank, which flows into the seat and side panels, which both flow into the new tailpiece. Some were taken by the styling, but overall, the styling limited the T5's popularity.

The frame on the 850-T5 is based on the California II frame, but it is fitted with a new swingarm that is the same length as that of the Le Mans III but wider, like the California II's. New forks are fitted, with 38-millimeter tubes, air-assisted dampers, and a narrower width (180 millimeters versus 195 millimeters). Rear shocks are Paolis, also air-assisted. American models were fitted with round-slide 30-millimeter Dell'Ortos and rubber manifolds, while Euro versions were fitted with solid-mounted square-slides. Brakes are 270-millimeter non-floating discs all around. Hand controls are of a new type with integral throttle, trapezoidal master cylinder, brake lever, and switches on the right, and integral switches and clutch lever on the left. Dual-tone air horns like those on the Le Mans III are also fitted.

With its 16-inch wheels, the new T is lower and much lighter steering than the old. Most reviewers bemoaned the loss of the ground clearance and steering stability of the old Ts. *Cycle Guide* magazine tested the 850-T5 in November-December 1984 and really didn't have many positive comments. The most enthusiasm the reviewer could muster was to comment that "The 850-T5 is unique." Nevertheless, some riders loved the T5. "That's a sweet-riding machine," said dealer Russ Heulitt of Two R's Moto Guzzi. "The 16-inch wheels gave it a low profile, and it rocked around corners real easy."

In early 1984, a revised 850-T5 (series II) was released, with more bracing and a longer steering head on the frame, a single fork spring per tube (instead of two), a silver paint option, and German-market versions were given a proportioning valve on the linked brakes and a larger rear caliper.

Late in 1984, the 850-T5 (series III) received another package of updates, including an 18-inch rear wheel, longer centerstand and sidestand (relocated below the shift lever), vents for the cylinder heads, blue-black paint on the rocker covers, Koni shocks, a return to two fork springs per tube (different springs, though), a small windscreen for the fairing, plus round-slide Dell'Ortos, and a brake proportioning valve on bikes for all markets. With the change to the 18-inch rear wheel, the 850-T5 gained back some lost ground clearance but sales never really improved because the styling appealed to the few. Even so, the civilian 850-T5 stayed in production through 1987, and the police version into the 1990s.

Two police versions were offered, the 850-T5 P.A. (with a unique version of the SP II frame-mounted fairing) and the 850-T5 F.F. Police (with a special version of the SP III frame-mounted full fairing).

SP II

Guzzi's sport-touring SP was the last of the line to get the upgrade to the new engine, when the SP II was introduced for 1984. The new SP was basically a 850-T5 chassis (late type, with 18-inch rear wheel) fitted with the 949-cc small-valve, square-head engine and the fairing from the SP. Two color options were offered: dark metallic brown, with red-and-gold trim, and smoky quartz metallic, with blue-and-gold trim. SP IIs for the U.S. market were fitted with 30-millimeter Dell'Orto PHFs and rubber manifolds; the first ones for other markets were fitted with 30-millimeter VHBs and metal manifolds.

Like the previous SP, the SP II was a fast, comfortable long-distance touring machine, this time slightly faster because the square-head engine put out slightly more power than the old round-head. As on the other big Guzzis with the 16-inch front wheel, the quick steering that resulted proved somewhat disturbing to long-time Guzzi riders.

The SP II continued virtually unchanged for 1984–1985. In 1986, an 18-inch front wheel was substituted for the 16-incher, restoring the more stable handling of the earlier SPs. Starting in 1987, a new alternator, made by Saprisa, was introduced. At the end of the production run, new hand controls were introduced. The SP II was replaced at the end of 1987 by the SP III.

Le Mans 1000

The next update to the Le Mans, the Le Mans 1000 (often referred to as the Le Mans IV), was announced in November 1984, for the 1985 model year. This new model was available initially in red and white, both with red wheels.

The signature feature of the new machine is a 949-cc engine in Le Mans tune. Compared to the other versions of the square-head, the Le Mans 1000 heads have bigger valves (47-millimeter intake and 40-millimeter exhaust), so the combustion chambers were made larger in diameter and deeper to allow room for the valves. New pistons with a much higher dome and valve pockets were then fitted to raise the compression ratio to 10:1.

While the civilian 850-T5 was discontinued after 1987, a police version was built into the 1990s. Shown here is the 1988 fully faired version, with a fairing similar to that of the SP III. *Moto Guzzi*

The basics of 850-T5 styling were combined with the 949-cc square-head motor and the fairing of the 1000 SP to create the SP II, introduced for 1984. *Frank Wedge collection*

The camshaft is the B-10 cam from the 850 Le Mans race kit, and stiffer outer valve springs were fitted to accommodate the cam and heavier valves. These engines all had the vented heads and an updated breather system that returns scavenged oil to the engine through the cylinder-head vents. We'll refer to this engine as the "big-valve" engine.

The Le Mans 1000 was given a major restyle to bring its looks in line with the latest small sporting Guzzis (this time based on the Imola II, Monza II, and Lario). Styling of the Le Mans 1000, more than almost any other big twin, reflects the active hand of De Tomaso, according to Umberto Todero:

The solutions we used for the Le Mans 1000 were studied and approved by Mr. De Tomaso directly. Listening to suggestions from the commercial division, he imposed the 16-inch front wheel and the modifications to the front fork to be used with the reduced diameter wheel. . . . The motorcycle was thoroughly tested under De Tomaso's direct control, and he had some of the testers at his disposition in his Modena bureau.

Most of the restyling was on the rear end, with swoopy new sidecovers, seat, and tail section. But the front fairing was also subtly refined, with new streamlined turn signals on world-version models, but rectangular turn signals similar to those in the Le Mans III on the U.S. variant. The U.S. turn signals are certainly less rakish than those on the others, but they are also more practical. In a mild tipover or low-speed crash, the U.S. signals pop free and are seldom even damaged, whereas the Euro turn signals invariably break. Exhausts were in black chrome, and the rocker covers and disc carriers were finished in blue-black to match.

Part of the styling was a switch to what was then in fashion but has since been almost universally abandoned, the 16-inch front wheel. Lino Tonti described the change to the 16-incher as "the mode of the moment." Others have complained long and vigorously how it "ruined" the handling. Some liked the quicker handling, however. Another mode-of-the-moment change was the addition

of a plastic sump fairing, use of which forced relocation of the sidestand to the middle of the bike, just under the shifter.

The 16-inch front wheel required smaller brake discs (270 millimeters rather than 300 millimeters), but they are semi-floating on the Le Mans 1000. Hand controls and switchgear are like those on the 850-T5 series III. The integrated brakes are controlled by a remote-reservoir master cylinder. Suspension on both ends was improved compared to the Le Mans III, with 40-millimeter air-adjustable forks and Koni adjustable shocks. The frame was reinforced and fitted with the wider swingarm of the 850-T5 to allow a wider rear rim and tire.

Some love the updated look and some see entirely too much plastic. As a result, sales were good in some markets and poor in others. Also, for at least part of 1985, the U.S. importer had a curious policy: "To get a red one, you had to buy a white one, too," remembered Joel Gulbranson, who ran JRG Performance.

Reviews

Magazine testers, in general, thought it was a decent bike, but clearly gave the impression they were holding back on their criticism to avoid "beating up on the little guy." *Cycle* magazine tested it for March 1986 and seemed mildly impressed. Flying in the face of many later criticisms about stability of the model, *Cycle*'s tester liked the Le Mans 1000's high-speed handling, commenting that "the factory's front-end alterations have paid big dividends without exacting noticeable penalties in ultra-high-speed stability: winding through deserted back-country roads, the 1000 glides along with nary a bobble, displaying a touch of floatiness only at speeds well in excess of 100 miles per hour." He also commented on Guzzi's "aggravating tradition" of very stiff throttle springs and clunky shifting. Performance was judged as "respectable," but much better than previous Guzzis, with a quarter-mile time of 12.48 seconds at 109.46 miles per hour, which is slightly faster than the same magazine was able to wrest out of the Le Mans III. Overall, though, they thought it was a good value for the retail price, which was $4,685, about the same price as many Japanese 750s of the day.

Stability Problems

Some customers complained about stability problems caused by the change to a 16-inch front wheel, so Moto Guzzi changed the triple clamps, beginning with number VV 1000165. The new triple clamps shortened the wheel base and lengthened the trail. As part of the update, the front fork received new (non-air-adjustable) dampers, bar-end weights were added, and the fender brace was redesigned. Moto Guzzi also put together a kit of parts to retrofit the updated parts to earlier machines. Later, the company made available a kit to retrofit an 18-inch front wheel, as well.

Some believe 16-inch wheels on Guzzis are the root of all evil. The author, however, has over 100,000 miles on two Le Mans 1000s (one, an early 1985 model, without the triple-clamp update) under all conditions, and never had any stability problems except those traceable to other causes. This is possibly due to luck and two exceptional machines, but the majority of Le Mans 1000 owners seem to have had similar luck. Most likely the major "cause" for these criticisms is simply that with the 16-inch wheel, the Le Mans steers like no other Guzzi. *Cycle* magazine in March 1986 said, "Long-time Guzzi riders will find the steering surprisingly, even startlingly, quick," and they're right. Simply put, the standard for sport-bike steering had changed since the 850 Le Mans of 1976, and with the Le Mans 1000, Guzzi tried to catch up. Even with the smaller wheel, though, the new Le Mans was on the slow end of the sport-bike steering scale—but at least it was back on the scale. Unfortunately, it was quick enough to alienate Guzzi traditionalists, but not quick enough to win over converts from other marques.

The other major "cause" of problems is not really a fault of the wheel, but is due to the fact that the smaller wheel is less able to mask handling faults that are really the symptoms of other problems. When properly set up, the Guzzi 16-inch front end works well. Ask Dr. John Wittner, who kept the 16-inch wheel (*without* the triple-clamp

update) on his 1985 AMA endurance-champion Le Mans racer.

So what are these other problems? The main culprit seems to be the frame-mounted fairing. At speed, it exerts a lot of pressure on the steering head, which is no problem if the fairing is centered exactly and pointing straight forward. If not, problems ensue. Also, the 16-inch front wheel is hypersensitive to tire pressure variation and requires relatively high pressure, 35–37 psi, depending on the specific tire type. Finally, choose tires carefully, because some give much more stable handling than others. Wittner found the Metzelers (both the Lazers and the company's racing slicks) to work best on the Le Mans 1000.

Le Mans 1000 SE

To commemorate 20 years (although it really was the 21st year) of the Guzzi big twin, the Le Mans 1000 SE (special edition) was released in the United States for 1987. To set it apart, it was given a close-ratio gearbox, a special red-and-white paint scheme with special decals, a red seat, black-painted drivetrain, black lower frame rails and foot-control castings, Pirelli radial tires, and Bitubo fork dampers. The SE carried a list price of $6,955, over $1,000 more than the regular Le Mans, and only 100 were imported. Many of these received corrosion damage in shipping, however. "All the nuts and bolts had grown a beard," according to sales rep Dave Hewitt.

Despite the updates, the SE really wasn't improved enough to justify its higher price, unless you

In late 1984 for the 1985 model year, the fourth version of the Le Mans was released, officially called the 1000 Le Mans, but unofficially known as the Le Mans IV. This 1985 Le Mans is owned by Nolan Woodbury, writer of the "Roadworthy" column for the *MGNOC News*. He has kept it remarkably stock, and it looks very clean after having been ridden from Arizona to the 1997 national rally in Washington State.

just had to have the special graphics. In fact, as a street bike, it is less practical than the regular Le Mans and more sluggish, because first gear in the transmission is noticeably taller, so a bit more clutch slipping is required to get it in motion. Magazine reviews of the day reported quarter-mile times more than 1 second longer than for the standard Le Mans. As a result of its high price and too-tall gearing, the SE sold poorly and some sat on showrooms for years. Further slowing sales, the corrosion-damaged machines were released for sale at $4,500, nearly $2,500 less than undamaged SEs.

Updates

For 1986, the fork dampers were changed from Paoli to Sebac units. For 1987, Bitubo fork dampers and bar-end weights were standard. Also for 1987, the headlight switch on U.S. machines was hard-wired on with the ignition. The "Marlboro-pack" red-and-white bodywork used on the SE was also available in Europe as a color option on the standard Le Mans 1000.

In early 1988, a substantially revised Le Mans 1000 entered production, with a new frame-mounted fairing, revised forks, new front fender, new switchgear, a true proportioning valve on the inte-

grated brakes, and an 18-inch front wheel. Color choices were red with red wheels or two different versions of red, white, and black combinations (one with red wheels and black seat and the other with white wheels and a red seat). Frames on most were black (even the removable lower rails). Later in 1988, adjustable Bitubo dampers were phased in as stocks of the old nonadjustable units dried up. This model didn't reach the United States until late in 1988, for the 1989 model year. With these changes, the handling problems seemed to disappear, as much the result of the frame-mounted fairing as the 18-inch front wheel. Often referred to as the "Le Mans V" (not an official designation), this version of the updated Le Mans remained in production through 1989.

In 1990, a revised version of the "Mark V" was released, with a new fairing with integral instruments, ignition switch on a new top fork cover, and new, longer forks. This model is sometimes referred to as the "Le Mans V NT." Various paint combinations were used on this model, some black with black frames and pearl-white wheels (no polished edges on the wheels), some red with red frame and wheels (wheel edges polished), and some of the late ones with regular "white" chrome exhaust pipes and mufflers (early mufflers with red-painted end caps

Dr. John Wittner's Le Mans 1000 racer. He got the first Le Mans 1000 brought to the States and began modifying it to compete in the AMA's Heavyweight Endurance class against the 1,000-cc Japanese fours. Though the team ran the supposedly awful 16-inch front wheel all year, they made many other modifications, including a stainless-steel two-into-one exhaust that Dr. John helped develop (built by EPA) and a large tank hump to hold extra fuel and allow a double-dry-break filler system. The hump was added just before the 1985 Paul Revere 250, and the extra fuel capacity was one of the key elements to their victory in that race. *Frank Wedge collection*

and later with black-painted caps). Also, some late machines were fitted with the close-ratio gears of the Le Mans SE, perhaps to use up excess stocks. In October 1992, the last Le Mans 1000s, the Le Mans Ultima Edizione variants, were produced. Only 100 were made, and each came with a number plaque affixed and a certificate signed by Alessandro De Tomaso and Paulo Donghi. Colors were the same red used on the Daytona and black. These 100 special machines were the exclamation point at the end of a 17-year run for the Le Mans as a model.

Dr. John, 1985

After their championship season in 1984, Dr. John Wittner and team were back, this time with a Le Mans 1000, partial sponsorship from Maserati North America, a superbly efficient and organized team, and a new rider in the stable, Larry Shorts.

With the new Le Mans, the team was bumped up to the AMA's Heavyweight Modified class, and Wittner did a lot of modifying over the course of the season. Externally, the goal was still to keep the bike as stock looking as possible. Wittner kept the 16-inch front wheel and Guzzi forks, but modified the forks to take conventional damper rods. The engine was very highly modified, with longer Carillo rods (keeping the stock stroke), aluminum plates under the cylinders, lightened crankshaft, forged pistons, porting work, timing gears, special exhaust, special camshafts and valve springs, and Mikuni carbs. Said Wittner, "We were really starting to put money into it."

Valvegear problems plagued the engine at first, the natural result of trying to run the engine at 9,000 rpm for a full six-hour race. As usual, Wittner worked at the problem, mostly at club races in between endurance events, until he found "solutions" (perhaps his favorite word). After a few races, the engine had been developed to the point that it put out 95 horsepower at the rear wheel, sustainable through a whole race.

Ed Davidson and Kathleen Childress renamed the team after the doctor and went after sponsors, signing Mobil Oil and Le Coq Sportif, among others. "The distributor of Le Coq liked motorcycles and thought some racing exposure would be interesting," said Dr. John. "It wasn't a big-money sponsorship, but it sure got the team looking good." (Le Coq supplied all their track clothing.)

With the increased power and torque of the long-rod motor, the Guzzi was able to stay with the big-bore Japanese bikes in its class and was reliable enough to outlast them too, if the team stuck to its strategy. According to Wittner:

> We would have a meeting before every race, and Ed Davidson would explain to the riders that if they crashed the motorcycle they would die—we would kill them. And therefore they were to take no

The author's Le Mans 1000, with a lot of aftermarket equipment, including Astralite wheels, Forcella Italia fork, and an Agostini fairing. *Michael Dregni*

> risks. We actually forbid them from leading races until the last five minutes of the race. We wanted them to stay 20 or 30 seconds back, not push the pace of the race, and not be on the other riders' minds, to be just invisible until it was time to win. You only have to be first on the last lap.
>
> Our philosophy was that the motorcycle should stay on the track. We weren't changing brake pads or tires or anything. Pit stops were for fuel only. The whole strategy was based on keeping on the track. Let the other teams change their tires and screw up by not being able to get their axle in, and it happened.
>
> At that time, the biggest competition was the new 1,000-cc Honda [VF1000R]. Honda wanted very badly to win races with their new bike, and they never did against us. They waited until after the last race of the year to introduce it, but they had to do it without claiming any endurance wins. It burned up its brakes and overheated and crashed and did all sorts of things but win.

In the end, Wittner and friends beat the Hondas and Kawasakis for the overall championship, and there were several notable victories along the way. One in particular still makes Wittner shake his head in wonder:

> At Mid-Ohio, we were winning the race when the driveshaft snapped; this is the only time this had ever happened. With the dumb luck that we had that season, the race was red-flagged on that same lap. [Greg Smrz thinks the race was red-flagged to allow them a chance to get back in the race.] We replaced the driveshaft in about five minutes and were ready for the restart.
>
> They started the bikes in single file—there were 80 entrants—and we were the last bike on the grid. Greg could not even see the start line he was so far back. Ed Davidson and I were standing with him, waiting for the start to come off. Greg said, "You see all those motorcycles?" We said, "Yeah." He said, "I'm gonna pass every single one of them in one lap." Eddie Davidson said, "Yeah, Greg, you

can do it," but you know, we didn't believe it for a second.

The race starts up, and normally the guys that are in the back are the slowest guys. Greg starts moving up at a pace I can't believe. Before he crosses the start-finish line, he's passed like 30 of the riders. He goes into turn one and probably bumped about six people off his line and into the grass, and this was where he got his nickname: "Bam Bam." He had no mercy, none whatsoever. He didn't look for opportunities to push people off the track, but if he had to get past someone, he'd go on the inside of them, pick the Guzzi up so the cylinder would hit them somewhere near their center of gravity, so they'd just go shooting off the track. It would never upset the Guzzi. Greg thought that was one of the Guzzi's big advantages for his style of riding. He said, "Yeah, it's really hard to do with a regular bike, but with a Guzzi you can just get rid of these people at will."

So anyway, he comes around start-finish and he hadn't passed 79 motorcycles; he'd passed 78 of them, and he was about 20 feet behind the other really fast entry, which was the Lockhart Kawasaki with Wendell Phillips riding. When he came around the next time, Greg was about a hundred yards in front of Wendell—and Phillips had a 1,000-cc Kawasaki. Greg just kept going and won the race. Greg was unbelievable. The guy had deep resources, that's all I can say.

Greg Smiz gives the thunderous sound of the Guzzi much of the credit for getting by all those

other riders: "That Guzzi sounded like a stock car. All you had to do to unnerve anyone in front of you was roll off the throttle right when he was at the apex of his turn. He'd sit up and go straight off the track."

After that ride, the team presented Smrz with business cards with the nickname "Bam Bam" on them.

Another notable victory was at the Paul Revere 250, a night endurance race at Daytona. This was a very prestigious race because it was held the night before the Firecracker 400 NASCAR race, and lots of TV crews were present. Wittner didn't ride in this race, but he helped win it with innovation and clever preparation:

One of the advantages our Moto Guzzi always had was lower fuel consumption. We made some really careful calculations before this race and decided that we could win this race with a bigger fuel tank and only one fuel stop. I welded this big hump on the fuel tank to get the extra capacity. When we showed up at the race with the humped tank, everybody's eyes popped out because apparently no one else had thought of it. That hump really gave us an edge, and the riders ended up liking it because it was comfortable to rest on while tucked in at high speed. It also gave me a huge flat area for the double dry-break—and nobody used double dry-breaks until we started doing that. Nobody.

I did a bunch of testing, and I found out that with two dry-breaks I could dump a whole load of

Starting with the 1988 model, the Le Mans 1000 was fitted with an 18-inch wheel and a frame-mounted fairing. During the year, adjustable Bitubo dampers were added to the fork tubes. In 1990, the fairing was revised to include an instrument console. This is one of the optional paint schemes. *Moto Guzzi*

fuel in about 3 seconds, rather than the 9–10 seconds it was taking with a single dry-break. Everybody on earth started using them after that. To give a bit more range, we also packed our gasoline in dry ice and then put it in just before the start and topped it up after the warm-up lap.

We had a guy named Mark Smith who was a video cameraman and producer for everything from commercials to documentaries. He set up the lights for us, so we had better lighting in the pits than anyone else and halogen lights on our pit board so the riders could see it at night. I got sponsorship from Hella for the event, and we had a headlight that was huge and heavy, but the riders could see almost a half mile. It was so much better than anybody else's that bikes that were a whole lot faster were forced to follow the Moto Guzzi because they simply could not see well enough to go as fast as the Guzzi was going.

All these bikes were on the Guzzi's tail for quite a while, and then they started to make their pit stops. They all had to make two pit stops. When there was about 50 miles left in the race, some of the other team owners came over to our pits and asked, "Well, when are you stopping for fuel again?" We said, "We're not." Their faces fell because they knew it was all over. We won that race with about a minute in hand. And we crossed the finish line with an empty tank and just two ounces of fuel in the filters and lines. That win was a big experience for us, and we picked up a lot more sponsorship after that because all the TV crews were there for the NASCAR race.

Greg Smrz did much of the riding in the race and also attributes the victory to gadgetry and preparation:

At a track like Daytona, we didn't have the speed on top to run with those other guys. John was very smart about everything, so we beat them with brains rather than brawn. He's an absolute NASA engineer. That's where he belongs. It's lucky for everybody he's in the motorcycle business.

He rigged up paint-peelers for lights and made sure the generator system would handle it. We had the big quartz beam in the center, and massive lights on each side that we would turn on as needed. He had them hooked up to the turn-signal switches, left and right. If you were going into a left, you'd turn on the left light, and for a right turn the right light. When you hit the straightaway, you could turn them off.

By the final race of the season, at Daytona, Wittner's team was almost assured of taking the championship, if they finished. They coasted through the race and took the overall AMA endurance championship. As recognition for its outstanding achievement, the whole team was given the Sportsman of the Year Award.

Wittner's team would be back in 1986, but they found it ever more difficult to compete against

Moto Guzzi's first serious attempt to jump into the big cruiser market was the California III, which debuted in 1987. Shown is a 1990 model, equipped with a catalytic converter and chrome panels on the fenders. *Moto Guzzi*

In 1989, Moto Guzzi attempted to turn the California into a big touring bike, with the release of the fully faired version shown. It was an excellent touring machine, but it was totally overshadowed by the six-cylinder Honda Gold Wing released in 1988. *Moto Guzzi*

the improved Japanese four-cylinders. The team was also burning out after two full seasons of racing, and Wittner's bank accounts were running dry. They dropped out partway through the season, and Wittner began developing a new frame and a sprint-racing motor to compete in twins racing. This story will be told in chapter four.

California III

In late 1987, Moto Guzzi released the California III, a completely restyled machine that came much closer than any previous Guzzi to capturing the custom Harley style. To its credit, Moto Guzzi designed an "honest" cruiser, not trying to hide the truth of what they were emulating, but also not re-

In late 1987, Moto Guzzi came out with a really great sport-tourer in the form of the SP III. It was powered by a 949-cc engine with the heads of the Le Mans III, and electronic ignition. The fairing was all new, and frame mounted. Unfortunately, the SP III sold poorly because of its high price (at least in the United States).The SP III fairing provides great wind protection for the rider, without making the motorcycle look overly heavy. It is a surprisingly swift and comfortable machine. Perhaps it's time for a V11 SP?

sorting to such fakery as chromed plastic covers to emulate the functional air cleaner or other key styling cues of the Harley-Davidson. And it is also a very functional bike, with better performance, handling, and brakes than on most of its competitors. It soon proved to be Moto Guzzi's best selling model in most markets.

Over the years, the California III was issued in a bewildering variety of variants, with three versions of the square-head engine, in various states of dress, with spoke wheels or cast wheels, and in many color combinations for various markets, including an Anniversary Edition (in both injected and carbureted versions for different countries, all with a brown leather seat, special metallic paint, a commemorative badge on the front fender, a numbered plate on the steering head, and a certificate signed by De Tomaso and Donghi) to commemorate the 70th anniversary of Moto Guzzi, in 1992. The four basic models are the world-market standard California III (early machines; has high handlebars, a shield, crashbars, and bags in most markets), U.S.-market standard model (early machines; without windshield and bags), the LAPD (a U.S. model that was the same as the world-market standard model, with bags and a windshield), the Classic (introduced in 1990, with lower bars but without shield, bags, or crashbars), and the F.F. (fully faired, starting in 1989), each in injected and carbureted versions.

Externally, much more was new on the California III than was borrowed from the California II, and all the new parts gave a much more chopper-esque look. Instead of conventional dual petcocks below the gas tank, the California III is fitted with a gas shut-off knob that is integral with the right side panel (except no shut-off on fuel-injected models) and a low-fuel warning light on the dash. Atop the tank is an updated version of the old hinged chrome cap from the 1970s, but the new version has an integral key lock. The seat is deeply stepped, with separate sections for rider and passenger and a short sissy bar at the rear. Tires are skinnier at the front than at the rear, and the fenders are fat and valanced. New forks have the 40-millimeter tubes of the Le Mans, but longer to add to the chopper look. Atop those tubes is a new instrument cluster with chromed covers for the speedo and tach.

The California III wasn't just a fashion plate, however. Underneath all that new bodywork is a small-valve square-head Guzzi engine with 30-millimeter carburetors. In 1991, the medium-valve SP III engine became standard in most markets. Some U.S. California IIIs in 1991 and 1992 were given a big performance boost with the big-valve motor and 40-millimeter carbs of the Le Mans 1000. In 1993, the medium-valve engine became standard on all U.S. variants. Fuel injection was also optional for some years in all versions. The Weber-Marelli fuel-injection system on these machines used 36-millimeter throttle bodies, and the electronic control module is under the seat.

Engine and drivetrain finish varied on different batches of California IIIs. Most of the first ones were painted black, later ones were left bare aluminum, and still later, they were painted silver. Rocker covers are polished bright on all, except for some later fuel-injected models. The exhaust is chrome plated and has unique mufflers, slash-cut at the rear on small-valve variants; medium-valve variants are fitted with a different muffler having less upsweep. Givi hard bags replaced the earlier bags.

The frame is a variation of the classic Tonti design, with all the good qualities that come with it. Adjustable damping, adjustable spring pre-load, and an integral fork brace make the California III forks among Guzzi's best. Same for the triple disc brakes, 300-millimeter floaters in front and a 270-millimeter floater in the rear. Non-faired U.S. variant through 1990 and only the first European variants have slightly lower 6/32 rear-end gears and 20-tooth splines. All fully faired and 1992-on models have the standard 7/33 gears of the other models.

In an attempt to capture a piece of the luxury touring market, a fully faired version was offered starting in 1988, with a more highly styled version of the SP III fairing. Hard saddlebags and a top trunk are also standard. The fully faired California III is an excellent tourer. Unfortunately, it was also expensive, which hurt sales, especially in the United States.

"I had one of the fully faired ones," remembered dealer Ken Johnson, "and it sat around for three years—nobody wanted it. Eventually, they even sent out a letter telling how to take off the fairing and lowers so they'd sell." When even that didn't work, the price on the model was reduced by over $3,000, and it began to sell. "Once the price dropped to $6,000, I sold 14 or 15, in 1992 or 1993," remembered dealer Joe Eish. "I even kept one for myself."

Updates

In addition to the major variations listed above, hundreds of small updates were made to the various California III versions over the production run. There isn't room to list them all, but the following are some of the more meaningful: In April 1989, a new spring-loaded automatic timing chain tensioner was fitted, beginning with engine 032698, and the transmission hub and clutch plates were revised with deeper splines, starting with engine number 032542.

Starting in 1993, all engines got the Digiplex electronic ignition. This ignition varies timing based on engine vacuum and rpm. The hole in the crankcase formerly filled by the timer is covered by an aluminum plug.

The Mille GT was introduced in late 1987 as Moto Guzzi's new "standard" machine. Shown is a 1990 model, equipped with a catalytic converter. *Moto Guzzi*

SP III

In late 1987, Moto Guzzi introduced the SP III, the first truly meaningful update to its sport tourer since the original 1978 SP. Highlights of the new machine include electronic ignition, a frame-mounted full fairing, and a new Le Mans-derived medium-valve engine with 36-millimeter Dell'Ortos that put a lot more sport in the sport-touring equation and made the SP III the best long-distance, high-speed Guzzi ever built. Standard colors included white, gold, silver, and teal, all with red graphics.

The most apparent update to the SP is its full fairing, replacing the old handlebar-mounted upper fairing and frame-mounted lowers. Its plain design is optimized more for rider protection than for looks, but in terms of protection, it is unparalleled. American-market SP IIIs have a different windshield than on other versions. Other new features included turn-signal beepers, restyled side panels, splash guards, Velcro-attached kneepads, wider bars, restyled seat, Givi bags, no reserve on petcocks, but a low warning light on the dash, a proportioning valve for the brakes, and a fold-out handle for hoisting the machine onto its center-stand. Some Swiss-market SP IIIs have a smaller filler hole on the gas tank for unleaded-gas nozzles, because the exhaust system is fitted with a catalytic converter.

With this machine, Guzzi was aiming for riders of BMW's RT series. While Guzzi certainly didn't succeed in getting droves of Beemer jockeys to convert, it succeeded in building a motorcycle that is at least the Beemer's equal in every way. At least in the United States, the SP III bombed on the showroom floor. Most loved the bike and the improvements, but the price was too high—over $10,000. SP IIIs piled up until the price was eventually lowered. "Once they dropped the price, I could sell them as fast as I could get them ready," remembered dealer Ken Johnson. "They're still selling for more now than I was selling them for brand-new."

Mille GT (1000 GT)

The third model introduced in 1987 was the Mille GT, which was first built at the request of the German importer and homologated as a variant of the SP III, according to Ivar de Gier. Over the years, the Mille was updated in many ways, but the parts books group the changes into three series.

Only 250 of the first series were built, each with a numbered plate on the passenger hand rail behind the seat. These machines were fitted with a curious mix of parts, many of which seem intended more to use up old parts on hand rather than to give the machine any special character. These old parts include the skinny 35-millimeter air-assisted fork, "dished" brake discs, and the tubular crossover last used on the California II and the narrower swingarm last used on the Le Mans III. Atop the old-style fork is the Florida-series instrument cluster, with chrome covers on the tach and speedo and a fuel-level warning light on the dash. Not really an "old" part, but certainly a veteran, is the engine: the small-valve square-head with 30-millimeter Dell'Orto PHFs. Series I Milles were offered in black with black frame and red with red frame. They came with cast wheels, but wire wheels were available as an option.

Series II Milles have unique, flat, iron discs, the wider swingarm of the Le Mans 1000, Moto-plat electronic ignition, new handlebar switches, and an expansion-chamber crossover. Blue-green with blue-green frame and swingarm was added as a color option.

Series III Milles received the larger instruments and 40-millimeter fork of the California III. American models have a vent hose on the gas tank and an unvented gas cap. In 1991, Milles received the medium-valve engine with 36-millimeter Dell'Ortos. Some Swiss-market Milles have a smaller filler hole on the gas tank for unleaded-gas nozzles, because the exhaust system is fitted with a catalytic converter. The Mille was discontinued at the end of 1991, replaced by the Strada.

1000 S (Mille S)

Moto Guzzi has a rich styling heritage. Unfortunately, the company hasn't been quite as successful as others in exploiting it. The first and only real attempt Guzzi has made thus far was released for the 1990 season, in the form of the 1000 S, a

Le Mans 1000 styled to suggest the 750-S3, one of the styling high points of Guzzi history. According to Ivar de Gier, this model was also built at the request of the German importer.

To make this modern replica, Guzzi fashioned a whole package of new bodywork styled after the Sport and S3 parts, including gas tank and sidecovers, seat and grab rails, taillight and bracket, chrome-plated fenders and headlight bucket, spoke wheels (cast optional), and a lot of polished and chrome-plated parts to complete the early-'70s look. The tank and sidecovers are painted with classic S3 racing stripes, in bright green or red-orange. On green-stripe models, the frame and swingarm are also painted green.

Most of the 1000 Ss came from the late Le Mans 1000, including the frame (although the rear sections differ), big-valve engine, Bosch alternator (some late ones may have had the Saprisa alternator), Valeo starter, exhaust system (but bright chrome instead of black chrome), forks, shocks, and controls. The instrument cluster on the first batch of machines was similar to that used on the 750 S and S3.

With all those Le Mans parts, the 1000 S was as fast and good-handling as any Guzzi, but it was the retro styling that was of real appeal to a whole cadre of *Guzzisti* who thought that De Tomaso's stylists had been getting a little carried away in

With styling reminiscent of the 750-S3 and a full-on Le Mans engine (with dual-point distributor, 40-mm carbs, and upswept exhaust) and chassis, the 1000 S was a great mix of the best of the old with the best of the new when Moto Guzzi released it for the 1990 model year. The first version is shown, with the old T3-style instrument cluster. This was changed later in the year to the style shown in the next photo. Wire or cast wheels were both available. *Moto Guzzi*

the 1980s, releasing models that Richard Attenborough accurately summed up in August 17, 1990, *Australian Motorcycle News* as looking "like they'd been styled by a deranged, mutant Tupperware designer on downers." By contrast, Attenborough wrote that the "1000 S, like the S3, looks bloody glorious!"

Updates

Sometime prior to 1991, the instrument cluster housing was changed to a unique polished stainless-steel plate that holds the tach, speedo, and warning lights. In 1991, all European variants were fitted with the medium-valve SP III engine with Motoplat electronic ignition, 36-millimeter carbs, SP III mufflers (less upsweep), and Saprisa alternator. A catalytic converter was also available. American variants kept the big-valve engine (the medium-valve-engine 1000 S wasn't brought to the United States until 1993). In 1993, the Digiplex ignition replaced the Motoplat. What the medium-valve engine gave up in peak horsepower, it gained in midrange power and reduced maintenance.

Sales

Initially, the 1000 S found a ready market in Europe, but it didn't make it to the United States until about 1991. American sales were disappointing, however, and they slowed in other markets as pent-up demand for a retro sport Guzzi dried up. The 1000 S was discontinued after the 1993 model year. After it was discontinued and supplies depleted, a curious phenomenon occurred that was repeated in 1998 as supplies of the Sport 1100 disappear: Suddenly, it's in demand! The almost unanimous comment among U.S. dealers at the time was, "Everybody wanted them once they couldn't get them." Perhaps there's an opportunity here for Moto Guzzi, or at least a lesson.

Harley-Davidson makes selling motorized nostalgia look easy, but with the 1000 S Guzzi, learned that it isn't. Guzzi made three mistakes: First and most important, they selected a limited-production model to "nostalgize" rather than the best-selling model of the era. Second, they didn't quite get the styling right, losing the illusion of "long, lean, and low" of the original S3. Third, the motorcycle wasn't modernized enough to appeal to anyone but *Guzzisti*, who at the time accepted such "Guzzi-isms" as breaker points (on the big-valve engines) in the 1990s, an oil filter hidden by a sump and 18 screws, and a 12-pound flywheel. Of course, none of this reflects badly on the machine—but as a marketing experiment, it was flawed in concept, inadequately executed, and premature.

Strada 1000

The Strada 1000 was introduced for 1992 to replace the Mille GT as the basic stripper Guzzi. It is essentially an SP III relieved of its fairing and saddlebags and fitted with the instrument panel of the last series of Mille GT. Powered by the medium-valve square-head engine and fitted with adjustable 40-millimeter forks and full-floating brakes, it is a good-handling, peppy, competent machine. Unfortunately, its styling is also very plain, so it never really gained a strong following.

For 1993, the Strada got the new Digiplex electronic ignition in place of the Motoplat. It was discontinued in 1994.

For 1994, Moto Guzzi put the 1100 engine (first put into development for the 1100 Sport) in a revised California III chassis to create the California 1100. The larger engine made a good cruiser even better. Shown is the 75th Anniversary edition. *Moto Guzzi*

California 1100

Although cruisers are much maligned by the sporty-bike crowd, the worldwide market for cruisers outstrips the market for sport bikes by a considerable margin—three-to-one in the United States, for example. And the big trend in cruisers is, well, "bigger." With all the major cruiser manufacturers striving to exceed the 1,340-cc standard set by Harley-Davidson, Moto Guzzi had to up-size to compete.

For 1994, Moto Guzzi took a tentative step toward keeping up with the pack in the cruiser displacement race by releasing a larger version of its popular and uncommonly functional California line. The new machine, the California 1100, featured an enlarged version of the medium-valve V-twin, with a bore of 92 millimeters and a stroke of 80 millimeters to increase displacement to 1,064 cc. Because this larger Guzzi engine was first conceived for the Sport 1100, its development is discussed in chapter four.

Because of the bore-and-stroke changes, the crankcase and heads are about the only large engine parts that weren't substantially revised. The crankshaft is stronger and has a longer stroke. Rods are stronger and are used with new forged pistons to get a 9.5:1 compression ratio. The camshaft was completely redesigned, with more gradual opening ramps to quiet valve operation, and it lacks the worm gears for the tachometer and ignition timer drives. The basic California 1100 features 36-millimeter Dell'Orto PHF carbs and the Digiplex ignition. The injected version, the California 1100i, features a sophisticated Weber-Marelli system with twin 40-millimeter throttle bodies and integrated electronic ignition. The new engine offers even more of everything that made the Guzzi engine such a perfect cruiser powerplant—smoothness, torque, and a broad spread of power.

In all, Moto Guzzi claims more than 200 changes compared to the California III. Some of the changes are significant, and some are merely to add more custom touches to the styling. Here's a list of the notable ones: larger airbox, sump pan with an adapter to allow use of a larger oil filter, new taillight-and-turn-signal assembly, new front master cylinder with 11-millimeter piston (was 13-millimeter on the California III), chrome-plated brake discs, taller overall gearing, nitrogen-charged Bitubo shocks, Akront rims (2.5x18-inch front and 3.5x17-inch rear), revised 40-millimeter fork with anti-friction bushings at the top of the sliders and the bottom of the tubes, frame bracing below the transmission, key lock for the seat moved to the frame rail below and to the front of the left side panel and connected to the latch by a cable, restyled mufflers, "California 1100" or "California 1100i" side panel badges, chrome luggage rack, rear crash bars, and more chrome covers.

Injected 1100s for the U.S. market are fitted with charcoal canisters on the frame and a nonvented gas cap. Standard colors include anthracite with silver tank panels and fender tops, all black with red pinstripes, black with yellow tank panels and fender tops, and black with red tank panels and fender tops. In 1997, a special California 1100 was released to commemorate the 75th anniversary of the company (750 were made). Later color options include dark red with lighter red panels, dark green with black panels, black with red panels, and dark blue with ivory panels.

Changes

Sometime during the first year of production, a plug was added to the bell housing below the starter for a magnet to collect any metal debris thrown off from the starter or ring gear before it gets to the magnetic ignition pickup on the right side of the bell housing. In November 1994, the

For 1991 (in most markets; for 1993 in the United States), the 1000 S was given the medium-valve engine (with 36-mm carbs, electronic ignition, Saprisa alternator, and exhaust) out of the SP III. The new engine was down on top-end horsepower but made more midrange torque and required less maintenance.

Ducati-built alternator was replaced by one of higher output. Carbureted California 1100s from frame number KC 13840 through 14712 are fitted with connecting rods like those on the Sport 1100 and a re-balanced crank to match. Late in 1996, new tank transfers were fitted. On these, the eagle faces forward on both sides. The side-panel decal was also revised, reading "California" only (no "1100" or "1100i"). Side panels over the rear shocks were revised to rubber-mountings.

V11 EV

After four years of production, the already excellent California 1100 was substantially revised yet again into a new model, the V11 California EV (just V11 EV in the United States). With the EV, carbs are no longer an option.

According to Moto Guzzi, it took 151 changes to turn the old California 1100 into the new EV. It works so well as a *motorcycle* that after a 13-bike test, *Cycle World* magazine crowned the EV king of cruisers in March 1998. Said the editors, "The enthusiast's rap against cruisers is that they lack horsepower, brakes, suspension, and handling. Not so the EV."

So, what were the 151 changes? With the EV, Moto Guzzi finally gave up trying to manufacture its own forks, fitting 45-millimeter Marzocchi forks with separately adjustable compression and rebound damping. At the rear, twin WP shocks match the front suspension well. New BBS wire-spoke rims have thick flanges like those on the old Borranis, and the short, stiff spokes only penetrate the flanges so the rim itself is airtight for tubeless tires. Brakes are 320-millimeter Brembo Gold Line stainless-steel floating discs with four-piston calipers in front and 282-millimeter fixed rear disc with a two-piston floating caliper. The linked part of the brakes is improved with a new proportioning and delay valve. It has a sensor on the swingarm to sense swingarm attitude and proportion the proper amount of braking to the front and rear linked calipers. According to Guzzi's tests, the new brakes stop the EV from 100 kilometers per hour in half the distance, compared to the California 1100. These sport-bike-spec brakes give the EV the best brakes in all of cruiserdom. Unfortunately, the foot brake pedal has the same awkward positioning as on the California III and 1100. On the plus side, the single disc controlled by the front lever has truly useful stopping

The Corazzieri drive California-series bikes today. Shown here is a line-up of 1100i models in September 1995. *Moto Guzzi*

power. Improved throttle bodies (first seen on the 75th Anniversary Cal 1100i) give smoother throttle response and increased torque, and 1100 Sport connecting rods strengthen the new engine.

Cosmetically, the EV has much more chrome, perhaps too much. New chromed parts include the alternator cover, steering-head covers, exhaust-pipe shields, and trim on the sides of the front fender. Even the stainless exhaust is chromed. Styling is cleaned up through the use of a flush-mounted filler cap on the tank and the smaller Centauro instruments. The tank-top vent pipe used on some earlier U.S.-variant Californias was also eliminated. A police version of the EV is also offered, with the sump (with externally accessible oil filter and oil cooler) and footpegs from the Centauro.

Future EVs

If present rumors prove true, a new low-rider V11 EV will be released just about the time this book hits the market, in fall 1998. Look for longer, lower, more custom styling and a true fix for the awkward brake pedal on the EV. With this new machine, Moto Guzzi is making the logical split in its cruiser line, with the low rider for the "custom" crowd and the regular EV for Guzzi's traditional touring-oriented California-model buyer. If the styling's right on the new machine without degrading the EV's inherent performance and practicality, the low rider has great potential to win over a new cadre of buyers for the venerable California line and for the marque itself.

Overall, the EV has a more refined, mainstream cruiser look that should make Guzzi's most popular model even more popular. The real significance of the V11 EV and the other new models discussed in the next chapter is that they demonstrate that Moto Guzzi has the will and expertise to get back in the game and produce world-class motorcycles once again.

In late 1987 Moto Guzzi introduced their latest version of the California series, the V11 EV. The EV was crowned by *Cycle World* magazine as the king of cruisers in 1998. *Moto Guzzi*

CHAPTER 4

THE SPINE-FRAME TWINS
Daytona through
V11 Sport and the Quota

Parallel developments on each side of the Atlantic in the summer of 1986 set the tone for Moto Guzzi in the 1990s and beyond. In the United States, Dr. John Wittner, having grown dispirited with trying to make his Le Mans 1000 racer competitive in the endurance racing series his team had won the previous year, dropped out of the series and began developing ideas for a new chassis that he had scribbled on the backs of envelopes and on napkins whenever he found a spare moment. In Italy, Umberto Todero was slaving over a hot dyno developing a new engine.

By the end of 1987, when each had proven the quality of his work, Wittner and Todero, and chassis and engine, would be brought together by Moto Guzzi boss Alessandro De Tomaso to form a transAtlantic partnership that would ultimately kickstart a revival for Moto Guzzi. This chapter is the story of the development of Moto Guzzi's new generation of machines, which all began with the development of the Daytona.

Roots of the Spine Frame

A big part of that story took place during the 1987 AMA Pro Twins race season, during which Wittner refined the new spine-frame chassis on the track, with the help of rider Doug Brauneck. The racer was powered by a highly refined version of the two-valve-per-cylinder Le Mans engine. The best way to relate the story is to let the people involved tell it like it happened. The quotes that follow are based on many hours of interviews with Brauneck and Wittner. Wittner's side of the story begins in the summer of 1986.

The 1987 Race Engine

"After pulling out of the endurance series, I began developing the Battle of the Twins engine, testing it on local sprint races: Summit Point, Bridgehampton, wherever I could go, and I used the endurance-bike chassis as an engine testbed. In final form, it was a short-stroke, big-bore, 70-millimeter stroke, 95-millimeter bore Moto Guzzi to turn 10,500 to 11,000 rpm. That's what I figured I had to do to make it competitive with Gene Church and Don Tilley's Harley-Davidson and Jimmy Adamo and Reno Leoni's Ducati. I was getting the kind of horsepower I wanted, and the bike was fairly fragile, but it would stay together at 10,500 and occasionally 11,000.

The Spine Frame

"Off the track during 1986, I was developing the frame that eventually became the first Daytona frame. I designed the frame in about two or three months, while there was still good weather around Pennsylvania. Then I built the frame with the assistance of a local race-car builder called S&W Race Cars. They were really clever and helped me in every way imaginable. I machined and fabricated most of the pieces, with the help of a guy who was very important all along the way, Jack Holloway, who runs a business called Holloway Machine Shop.

"The frame sideplates are central to the whole frame design. I chose that design for a number of reasons. First, the frame's bolted together because it's an experimental frame, so I wanted to leave the possibility of changing the engine position, the swingarm position, and just about every parameter of geometry you can imagine. One of my objectives, and it was a necessity, was to build a new motorcycle based on this Guzzi engine that would not require any new castings whatsoever because I didn't have the kind of relationship with the factory that would permit me to make a new gearbox casting to fit my swingarm; it just wasn't in the cards.

"I had worked out the frame mentally over a long period, sketching it out on the backs of envelopes in my spare time. I knew that was the direction I wanted to go in. I took a lot of inspiration

Rear frame sections of the single- and dual-seat models differ enough that the tailpiece of the single-seat version can be used on the dual-seat version, but not vice versa. The prototype Daytona had its air scoop on top of the tailpiece, but it was moved to the sides on the production machines because the original design made too much noise.

For 1987, Dr. John Wittner and Doug Brauneck campaigned a one-off Guzzi in the Pro Twins GP class against a factory Harley, Bimotas, and Ducatis. The engine was a highly modified short-stroke 1,000, fitted into a monoshock frame developed by Wittner and built by Maserati. Surprising everyone, they won the championship. Here he passes Bimota-mounted Dale Quarterly (32) and Ducati-mounted Jimmy Adamo. *Frank Wedge collection*

from a frame that was used on a KR Harley-David-son that was built by Jerry Branch in the 1960s. It was a short-stroke KR with a big, single backbone tube and welded sideplates. It was also inspired by the Harley Sprint frame.

"I made my plates out of aluminum, and there were three reasons for the holes in them: One, to save weight; two was I wanted to be able to support the motorcycle very quickly on stands, and all you had to do was shove a bar through there; and third, I loved it aesthetically. Those holes are closed on the latest Sports. It's too bad. They were a direct visual link to the racers, and they were a great place to stuff a sandwich.

Meeting with De Tomaso

"When I was just starting the frame design, De Tomaso told George Garbutt [manager of Maserati North America] to get me to Italy. He wanted to talk to me because he had been very impressed with what we'd done with the endurance racing. So I went over to Modena with George for a week, and

I got my chance to talk to De Tomaso. He asked me how I was winning all these races. I told him that the bike wasn't that fast, that we had done it with impeccable organization and race strategies that worked out better than anyone else's, but that I wanted to change to sprint racing. I showed him my sketch for the frame. He said, 'I like it, and we'll help you build it. We'll get George to pay for it.' George didn't like that very much. I said, 'Oh boy, great. Another year of racing.'

"Unfortunately, the money was very slow in coming. In fact it never came until probably two days before Daytona 1987. I built that whole thing, and I'll tell you I was really sweating at this point. I was in debt to everyone, and I must have had five credit cards maxed, but there was no way I was going to stop. The money from Maserati covered a bunch of the development cost, but there wasn't any room for a salary for me. I did have enough to start paying Doug, though. And there was no money for anything extra either. In 1987, we still drove around in a piece-of-junk GMC van with 250,000 miles on it.

Daytona 1987

"Anyway, I finished that motorcycle at 1:00 in the morning, the night before practice started at Daytona, and I was in West Chester, Pennsylvania, in Bob Griffith's garage. I was so tired I was on my knees. For a month I had been working 20 hours a day. I was really at my last physical resources when I got the bike finished. I never started it, never rode it one single foot. I put it in the old van, loaded up with every spare part I had and all the tools and drove straight through. I don't know how the van made it there; it must have been carrying 8,000 pounds, and it was just a half-ton van. I got there just as registration was closing, I mean just a few minutes ahead of time, and met Doug Brauneck.

"We went out to practice the first day, and the press was immensely interested in the motorcycle. It went well in practice, the speeds were good. I built that motorcycle with Daytona in mind, which was why it was eventually named the Daytona, although Santiago De Tomaso selected the name. We took sixth at Daytona that year, and to say I was pleased is a huge understatement. The bike had never been ridden one foot before we took it to Daytona.

"It had a very low seat height, and the engine was parallel with the ground—and this was the last of my bikes that did have the parallel engine because we were running into some problems with U-joint angles. The motorcycle goes better with the engine parallel to the ground, by a bunch. The tradeoff was that it had ground-clearance problems and had insufficient swingarm angle in the rear, so I had to use unusually stiff suspension in the rear of the bike. But in the end, as a chassis, it was able to get around a racetrack faster than any of the later versions.

"After Daytona, we still had major work to do preparing the motorcycle for the Pro Twins season. Doug was a great development rider, and that chassis underwent major geometry changes as a result of Daytona and the testing he and I did together."

When asked about it, Brauneck deflected much credit: "After the new bike at Daytona, I didn't really contribute anything new. Doc credits me with being a great development rider, but in reality, Doc asks the right questions. The real value in a development rider is in giving honest answers and not making up something just because you want somebody to think that you did feel a change."

Refining the Engine

Wittner continued: "The more immediate problems were with the engine, however. I worked very hard with another very, very important person in this story, and that's Manfred Hecht from Raceco, to develop the short-stroke [70-millimeter] motor. He did all of the cylinder-head work for all our motorcycles, from the beginning of the endurance racing. Manfred devoted an enormous amount of time developing cylinder heads and special cylinders

with 95-millimeter bores and iron liners and modifying engine cases.

"A pushrod engine turning that kind of rpm has some notable, disturbing vibrations in the engine and the rest of the valve train. That motor was fragile, but I was only forced to use the back-up motor one time, though, and I hated to do that. The backup motor didn't have the fabulous set of cylinder heads that we developed for the short-stroke version, which had downdraft ports that didn't even resemble the originals. The chambers and ports were created by welding them up and recutting them. I did the chamber, and Manfred did the ports. They flowed so much more than a standard set, but it took me so long to produce that set that I didn't have time to build a second set.

"That engine broke valve springs frequently, so I put in a new set before each race. It would also bend pushrods occasionally. Unlike the endurance motors, I had to tear the sprint motor down after every race. We could usually get by for a whole weekend on the engine's basic structure, but many times between Saturday and Sunday I'd change pistons and cylinders. It went against my nature to build fragile engines, but we got it more and more reliable as the season went on.

Dr. John Wittner working on the 1987 racer. Unlike the endurance-racing engines he tuned for the 1984 and 1985 championship seasons, the engine in this racer needed constant attention to keep from breaking the valve gear. *Frank Wedge collection*

While Wittner was developing the chassis on U.S. race tracks, Umberto Todero was developing the four-valve-per-cylinder engine that would power the next generation of Dr. John racers, and ultimately, the Daytona. Shown here is a prototype Daytona engine. A camshaft resides on the inboard side of each cylinder head, and each is driven by a separate toothed belt. Note the external oil filter, which was not fitted to production Daytona engines. *Moto Guzzi*

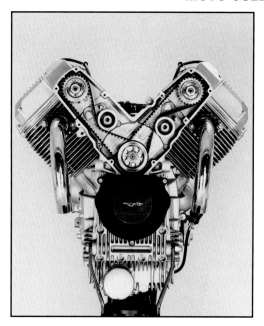

First Win

"Our fourth race was Loudon. [The second was at Road Atlanta where they took second, and the third was at Brainerd where they also took second, giving Wittner and Brauneck a one-point lead over Jimmy Adamo and the Reno Leoni-prepared Ducati.] Doug led that one start to finish."

Remembered Brauneck: "Without a doubt, one of the greatest races of my whole career was at Loudon. It was the first race I won on the bike, and it was also my first win at an AMA national. I was racing with Dale Quarterly, Jimmy Adamo, and Russ Paulk. We had a race-long battle—Jimmy and Russ on Ducatis and Dale on a Ducati-powered Bimota—but they never could get by me. We really showed them how good a Guzzi could be."

Vise Grips at Laguna Seca

Wittner again: "We won again at Road America and then took second at Laguna Seca. We probably would have won at Laguna, but our clutch cable broke [the barrel end of the cable fell off, according to Brauneck] just literally a minute before the last moment left to get positioned on the starting grid. There was *no* time to change the cable so I cocked the clutch with a Vise Grips.

"Fortunately, Doug qualified in a position that put him on the starting grid next to the pit wall. The idea was that Doug would hold it at 9,000 rpm and pop the Vise Grips when the flag dropped, hopefully launching them in my direction. I had him cover this thing with his arm and his hand—he looked like he was sleeping—because I didn't think the officials would let us do it. There was no way we were gonna be left out of this race."

Remembered Brauneck: "At the starting grid, I just held the throttle wide open. When the sign went sideways, I popped the lever, and it was like a drag-race start. I smoked the rear tire and it started sliding sideways. Of course, I had only one hand on the handlebar at the time. After that little burnout, I was damn near the last guy off the line. I had to pass a lot of people, and by the time I got in second place, there was no way I could catch Marco Lucchinelli, but I almost matched his lap times once I got past traffic."

Crash at Mid-Ohio

Wittner continued: "We crashed out at Mid-Ohio. I didn't see the crash itself because it was in the curve before start-finish; I only saw the bike come tumbling end over end. Later, I saw a photograph of Doug just before the crash. The bike had flipped him off on an almost high-side. In the photo, Doug was on his knees, with his hands still on the bars trying to steer out of it and get back on. When he got one knee back on the bike, it endoed. Nobody ever tried harder to save a motorcycle."

The crash is still vivid in Brauneck's mind: "I was sliding the rear tire out of the carousel, and I slid it a little too much. It began to high-side, but I held onto the bars and ended up on my knees on the left side of the motorcycle. I leaned the motorcycle to the left to get it through the corner, and then I tried to crawl back on. As I pulled myself on, I ended up giving it a handful of throttle, so it took off, and I began to slip off again. As I was slipping off, I gave it even more throttle and I couldn't quite catch up to the motorcycle. If I had had the presence of mind to let go of the throttle and grab the fuel tank, I probably could have got back on."

Wittner again: "Doug, having filled-in during 1986, knew about my attitudes about crashing. I'd get in a bad mood every time because I hated working with fiberglass and fixing fairings. I wanted to win this championship, and I realized that just as in endurance racing, staying on the track and finishing every race is much more important to me than winning every race, and I constantly reminded Doug not to take chances. In fact, I paid him the same bonus for winning as for finishing third because I really believed in this strategy, and it worked.

Sears Point and the Championship

"By the last race of the year, Sears Point, we were far enough ahead in points that I told Doug to just cruise because we didn't have to make much of a showing to win. We came in third, and the championship was ours. Most people don't remember a year later who won a particular race—particularly in the case of publicity that's useful for sponsors and manufacturers—but they sure remember who won the championship. So, the championship has an importance about 500 times greater than any race win."

According to Brauneck, "The last race of the year, Sears Point, was really fun and really funny, too, because the championship was basically ours unless we DNF'd. Jimmy (Adamo) was in second place, and we knew that he was a pretty aggressive rider and might resort to a few tricks, so I was under strict orders not to race with him, and not to win the race unless Jimmy dropped out.

"Anyway, we started the race. Jimmy was near the front, but I was quicker off the line and got by him right away. Dale Quarterly, Russ Paulk, and I took off and started putting on this incredible show. I knew exactly where I could pass them and feel that I could easily have won the race, except that I was under orders not to challenge them for the lead. We were all so close together that I couldn't get a good look at the pit board when I went by the start-finish line. It turns out that Jimmy was out and they had '26 OUT' [the signal that he could go for the win] on the pit board for the last two laps, but I didn't see it, so I just sat back there and finished third. It's too bad because I could have won that race without a problem. Anyway, we got the

championship, and if you ever see the pictures of the winner's circle, I doubt you've ever seen two guys happier than Doc and I."

Off to Italy

Wittner continued: "De Tomaso was ecstatic. The bike was so unusual and we led the series most of the year, so we made the cover of almost every single motorcycle magazine in the world during that season or shortly thereafter. At the end of that season, he said, 'Come to Italy, and bring the bike with you.'

"I stuck it in a crate and brought it over. He looked at the motorcycle and said, 'I think we should make these,' which is what I think he had in mind all along. They had a team of designers disassemble, dimension, and copy everything, including the motor. They even tested the motor on the dynamometer because they didn't believe me that the motor had 102 horsepower. They found that is exactly what it had at 10,200 rpm.

"Eventually, Moto Guzzi made three exact replicas of that motorcycle. One went to the French importer, one went to the German importer, and I

The prototype Daytona shown in 1989. This bike was fitted with 40-mm carbs (the street injection system wasn't yet ready, though it had been used on the racer since earlier that year) and a full fairing like that of Dr. John's racer. The air intake is on top of the tailpiece on the prototype. *Moto Guzzi*

With the production schedule already falling behind, the search for a suitable alloy for the Daytona cylinder heads pushed it over a year further out. But the time wasn't wasted. Chief Engineer Paulo Brutti and stylist Adriano Galarsi restyled the bodywork and refined it with the help of Dr. John, in the Guzzi wind tunnel.

don't know who got the third. The intent was to race them, but everybody managed to blow them up. It took a lot of maintenance to keep the valve-gear together on that motor; if you didn't do it, they'd just drop valves." According to Ivar de Gier, Klaus Kaspers rode the German importer's replica to second place at the Avus racetrack in Berlin. It was later raced at Assen, Holland, where it blew the bottom end, and was finally sold to a private party. The bike sent to the French importer was destroyed in a crash. And the third replica was kept in Italy.

Roots of the Daytona Motor

Occasionally, to break up the relative drudgery of designing updates to the production machines or conducting yet another round of homologation tests, De Tomaso would give Tonti and Todero an interesting project or two to develop, seemingly just in an effort to keep his two most creative designers from quitting the company out of sheer boredom.

Among the projects given to Todero was a four-valve-per-cylinder, double-overhead-cam V-twin using the existing crankcase. Before long it was on the dyno. "This engine was realized and tested on the dyno with excellent results concerning power and torque," according to Todero. Even so, development of the engine was stopped by De Tomaso because, according to Wittner, "the cylinder heads were too tall, and the exhaust came out the sides; it was not pleasing aesthetically."

Then Todero was turned loose again, with De Tomaso's direction to "use the V7 crankcases and build a four-valve with fuel injection and electronic ignition," remembered Todero. Since overhead cams had made his previous engine too tall, Todero settled on a scheme well tried on other machines faced with similar concerns over cylinder height: put the camshaft in the head, but not above the valves. Todero put a single camshaft on the inboard edge of each head to operate the four valves by a pair of cam followers acting directly on long, forked rocker arms. Drive to each cam is by a toothed rubber belt driven by a pulley on a jackshaft that replaces the old two-valver's cam. Since the cylinders needed to be redesigned anyway to move a couple of the cylinder studs, Todero made the new engine a true 1,000 by punching out the bore two millimeters to 90 millimeters, for a displacement of 992cc.

"De Tomaso preferred this engine because it was cheaper to build and it was less bulky too," said Todero, so De Tomaso gave the nod for further development. Todero built two prototypes and wrung them out on the dyno during 1987, with very promising results.

The 1988 Four-Valve Racer

Pleased with both Todero's new engine and with Wittner's chassis (not to mention the championship), De Tomaso brought the two together while Wittner

was in Italy in the fall of 1987. Wittner continued:

"De Tomaso told me that he wanted me to race with the four-valve motor. We went to the factory, and he told Todero, 'I want you to give one of these engines to John.' Todero screamed and yelled, as if De Tomaso had ordered Todero to give me one of his children. Todero was livid, but he sent one of the motors to me in Modena, and said, 'This is raw material; it needs a lot of development.'

"The engine he sent me was totally used up. It had been run hard on the dynamometer for over 200 hours. The heads were cracked, and the valve seats were falling out; there wasn't a single usable piece on that motor but the crankcases. I told De Tomaso, 'I can't use this' and he said, 'No problem; we'll make you new pieces.' They started making new cylinder heads, barrels, you name it.

"So I go back to Mandello and talk to Todero. He had calmed down by this point. You see, Todero gets mad all the time; it's just his nature, and now we get along fabulously. When I'm at Moto Guzzi I work with him every day. He's 75 years old. How many guys do you know that are still working 12-hour days when they're 75? And I think De Tomaso thought the whole thing was funny. He enjoys conflicts among his friends and employees. He thinks conflict is healthy.

"The cylinder heads weren't ready yet when I had to leave, so I just took the lower end home and set it up the way I wanted to, with a short stroke, Carillo rods, 95-millimeter bore, and so on. Essentially, I was going to put the four-valve heads on top of the two-valve bottom end, using all the tricks I had learned to keep the engine together.

Frame Refinements

"I wanted to change the engine position, rotate it up two degrees, which is the angle used on the Daytona and Sport 1100 today. I wanted to do this to gain ground clearance and to create a larger angle of the swingarm to gain an anti-squat effect that would allow me to use reasonable spring rates on the shock. Of course, there were tradeoffs. The motorcycle got higher. The Moto Guzzi engine has a rather large polar moment of inertia, so it's important to get that as close as possible to the polar moment of inertia around which the motorcycle leans as it turns, and this position happens to be low. There's an enormous advantage in the response and handling of the motorcycle when the two polar moments coincide, but for a street Guzzi you can't deal with the ground-clearance and ultra-rigid-suspension problems that go along with it. I know of other ways of solving that problem now because I've been studying the dynamics of shaft-drive motorcycles for more than 10 years, and I've developed some other solutions. Some of them we'll use at Moto Guzzi in the future."

A highly modified Sport 1100. To get rid of the midrange lean spot caused by the ram-air airbox, the owner has removed it and fitted an air filter to each carb. The Sport looks even better without the airbox—and more trustworthy, by Jay Leno's definition.

First Race: Daytona

"That short-stroke engine I'd been working on didn't get raced at Daytona. A normal bore-and-stroke [meaning 90 x 78-millimeters] engine got raced at Daytona in 1988 because there wasn't any time to prepare the short-stroke motor. Four-valve pistons needed to be made, and there was nowhere near enough time.

"The engine we raced was basically that first engine that Todero had given me, but with Carillo rods and a new set of cylinder heads that came to my house after I had already been at Daytona for about two days. I had Eddie Davidson waiting at my house for them. After they came, Eddie booked the first flight to Florida he could get. In the meantime, Crane cams had developed a set of camshafts for it, and we assembled the motor. I can't say enough about Crane, what they have done for Moto Guzzi, and for the development of this engine. Chase Knight and David Bly worked tirelessly.

"At Daytona that year, we had terrible problems with the valvegear. In fact, the valvegear was eventually revised as a result of what we learned that year. I didn't design that four-valve engine, but I contributed very heavily to its development—first in a year of racing in the United States and I carried all those solutions to Moto Guzzi Italy—and then in more than a year of testing and development at Moto Guzzi, working very closely with Todero.

"On the track at Daytona, the bike was about 2 seconds a lap quicker than the two-valve because it had enormous—but enormous—torque. Doug said that engine-wise, it was the easiest motor he ever had to ride in a race. It had more torque than anything he'd ridden on a racetrack.

"Unfortunately the frame wasn't straight. I spent most of the practice week trying to figure out how to straighten it. By the end of practice we had the bike going pretty well, and we took third. After having worked all winter and having taken the bike down there without even cylinder heads and having come in just behind Jimmy Adamo and Gene Church, I was pleased as punch at the third.

Short-Stroke Engine

"By the next race, Road Atlanta, I had built it into a short-stroke, with different cams, and it had a lot more power, a lot higher in the rpm range. I hadn't tested the short-stroke motor yet, but I found out later that it had 115 horsepower. I also built new telescopic forks with an external Koni shock absorber. We had been using Marzocchi forks and had been having a lot of problems with the damping and chatter. The new fork assembly really solved the chattering problem by making the forks much more rigid.

"We had lots of reliability problems, and they were all related to the valvetrain and the gear drive driving the cam belt. Up until the third race, which was Loudon, I kept snapping the jackshaft drive

According to Dr. John, the dual-seat version of the Daytona was built only because dealers insisted on it. This 1993 dual-seat Daytona is fitted with the Stage 1 racing kit. The alloy "boomerangs" on the Daytona provide a strong visual link to the Dr. John racers, and the hole in each provides a "great place to stuff a sandwich," according to Wittner. Guzzi enthusiast Jimmy Huggler calls them "Jay Leno's Holes," in reference to comedian and bike-lover Jay Leno's famous saying you can't trust a twin that light can't find its way through.

pins. We finally put three pins in, and that solved that. Then we had materials problems between the tappets and the cam lobes, and I couldn't get the tappets to rotate properly. Finally, with the help of the people at Crane, we figured how to modify them to rotate. My life then got a little easier.

"By that time I was lightening every rotating or reciprocating part to the maximum. Handling got better and better, but the four-valve engine is about 8 kilograms heavier than the two-valve engine. The cylinder heads, complete with camshafts, are considerably heavier than the two-valve heads, and the extra weight is carried high, increasing the polar moment of inertia further.

Another very trick Sport. Easily seen here are the Bimota mufflers and custom taillight. Harder to see in this view are the working altimeter and flush-mounted turn signals in the fairing, among dozens of other mods. The choice of script for the "Sport 1100" decals on the tailpiece is unfortunate because it is easily misread as "Spot 1100."

Monza

"In 1988, De Tomaso insisted that I bring the bike to Italy to race in an international twins race at Monza, which meant missing the final three races in the U.S. series. It was a very important race for Italy and all of the European market. Also, they'd heard about what we'd been doing in the United States, and part of it was they didn't believe how fast the bike was because they weren't winning any races with the two-valve replicas. De Tomaso wanted to see what I could do.

"Ducati showed up with Marco Lucchinelli and an early version of their 888. But our bike was fast. It was real fast. We led the whole race until about two laps from the end, when a spark-plug wire came out of the cap. At the time I was hot. I was incredibly embarrassed. I was flabbergasted. But we set the fastest lap of the day and got a huge trophy. And I was pleased that the motorcycle had gone as quickly as it did against competition like that."

Remembered Brauneck: "Lucchinelli qualified on the pole. I was on the second row for the start. When the race was about to start, Lucchinelli was looking down at his motorcycle—and then the start light came on. Basically, he was asleep at the wheel at the start, and I got the holeshot. I led the race until I broke down. They said he was right behind me in my draft—I don't look behind me when I race—until he broke and pulled off the track. I went around a couple more laps, and my bike broke.

"The people there were wild. Our tent was surrounded by died-in-the-wool, hard-core Moto Guzzi fans. At one point, one of them, just some guy, interrupted everybody and gave a speech about how much they appreciated everything we had done for Moto Guzzi."

Wittner continued: "Doug was unbelievable. To lead Lucchinelli for all those laps, I was impressed, and Moto Guzzi was too. They, including Todero, became much more interested in the development work I was doing and more confident that as a team we really were able to do development and chassis work on a level that was useful to the factory.

"After the Monza race, De Tomaso didn't say much; he's kind of like that—very reserved in his opinions. Notwithstanding that we didn't have any real results in the championship, we had delivered useful information to the factory about the development of the motorcycles. The motor was coming along nicely by the end of the season.

Daytona Prototype

"In September 1988, De Tomaso said, 'Come to Italy for a few weeks because we want to know firsthand what you have been doing with the motorcycle.' When I got there, he put me together with Santiago [De Tomaso] and said that they wanted to build this into a production motorcycle with the four-valve engine.

"One morning in December, I wake at the hotel I always stayed at, and I think—you know these startling thoughts—*Damn! I left my car at the airport two and a half months ago.* I hadn't even thought about it. Really. I called up my buddy Eddie Davidson and told him about it. I just had no idea what the bill was on that thing, so I asked him to check it out. And he goes down there and they want $700. Well, this was a 1971 BMW that I bought from my brother for $600. So, I told him to see what he could do because he was good at this stuff. He goes down there and tells them that I had a heart attack and that I couldn't come home and hadn't remembered about the car, so they settled for $50 or something.

"Anyway, the two weeks had turned into months. I came home for Christmas that year and went back right after to continue work on the original prototype of the Daytona and organize the modification to components and spare parts for the racing program. De Tomaso kept me there until near the end of February. I got home just in time to build the motorcycle for Daytona, 1989. I started to become much more involved and spend time at Moto Guzzi with Todero and began to work in the design office there.

"I was introduced to the people at Weber-Marelli, and we cooked up a fuel injection system. That's when I started doing a lot of dynamometer testing at Maserati; in fact, I spent six months there testing and mapping the fuel injection system, working with the wonderful people from Weber. And we picked up a bunch of horsepower. The horsepower now went up to 128.

"At this point it was clear to me that we really were moving toward development of a production model, but we were still also working on race development because it was quite clear to De Tomaso that without the racing, I wasn't interested because it's motorsports that fascinates and captivates me."

Developing the Street Prototype

Although Wittner and Doug Brauneck did some racing in 1989, most of the year was sacrificed to the effort to get the prototype of the Daytona on the road. De Tomaso wanted to have a prototype Daytona ready for showing in the fall of that year and on the market by 1990, and there was a tremendous amount of work to be done with very limited resources. Many different ideas were tried, including a new frame with a single-sided swingarm that had been worked on by Massimo Magliogli and later Lino Tonti. Ultimately, the street-going prototype that came of all these efforts used the spine frame developed for Wittner's racer.

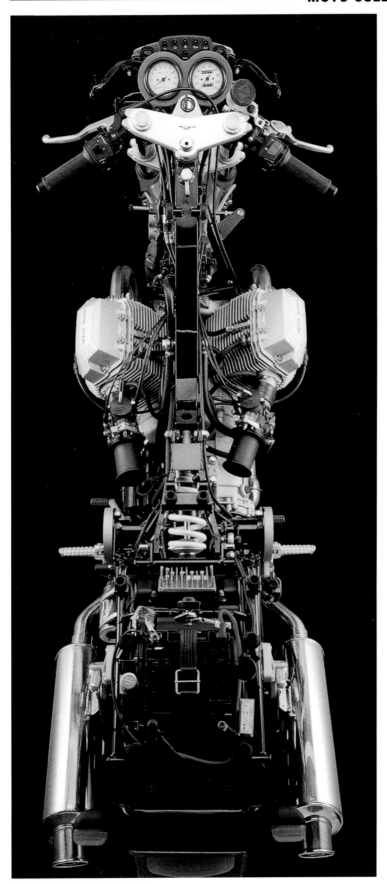

Prototype Road Frame

Wittner again: "The race-bike frame was copied for the Daytona, but the race motorcycle was in a very different setup than the road motorcycle. The whole motorcycle was tipped way forward in racing form. The front forks were shorter by 50 millimeters and the rear was higher by 35 millimeters or so, so that the wheelbase became much shorter, even though the steering-head angle of the frames was the same. That wasn't possible for the production version for a lot of reasons.

"And ground clearance was still one of the major considerations in the design. We had to incline the engine at two degrees, and still the fastest riders can make them touch the ground. That engine can't be placed even 1/8 inch lower. That two degrees may not seem like much, but if you rotate it level, the front of the engine drops 27 millimeters—that's a bunch—and besides that, you introduce another two degrees of angle on the universal joints. The way we ultimately will solve the problem is with the new six-speed with a lower output shaft.

"To get more clearance for wider wheels, we spaced the engine over 13 millimeters to the right. The handling effects are very, very minor because it changes the center of gravity of the bike, but the effects are much less than from spacing the wheel to the left.

Driveshaft Destruction

"We were having problems with the first Daytona shaft drive. At the time, our torsional testing equipment wasn't working, so I had no other recourse but to make shafts of reduced diameter and then have a test rider put the front wheel of the bike against a wall and keep popping the clutch on the thing until the shaft twisted. I put a line on the shafts so I could identify the point of twist and calculate just how much torsion it took to twist that so I could understand what our worst torque inputs were from the powerplant to the shaft. And I found out that they're monstrous—about 2.75 times the maximum calculated engine torque, with gear ratios included.

"I can't tell you how many gearboxes we exploded doing that. Usually, the shafts would twist because they were reduced-diameter shafts, but as I went up and up and made them more rigid, we started taking all the teeth off of first gear, and sometimes first gear would break in half and blow the whole side of the gearbox out, at which point everybody would clap and cheer. That was a down-home

An overhead view of a stripped Sport, from a Moto Guzzi brochure, shows the spine frame, rear suspension, pair of batteries, carbs, and the white-face speedo fitted to non-U.S. models (U.S. models have a blue-faced speedo). *Moto Guzzi* method of getting the answer. Somehow, people who love to build things also love to see them blow up now and then. We blow up engines on the dynamometer with great regularity, and everybody loves that. We put connecting rods through the cases just to make sure you won't do it.

Daytona Clutch and Flywheel

"The Daytona was the first one on which Moto Guzzi made a serious effort to lighten the flywheel. Since then, it's gotten successively lighter. I built some test rigs at Moto Guzzi to actually spin the flywheel to up to 16,000 rpm, which I consider a safe speed. The flywheels are fully machined so balancing isn't necessary.

"The Daytona got 10 springs in the clutch because it had a lot of power, and it needed them. It got really difficult to pull in the lever, so I looked at ways of reducing the lever effort. The geometry of the lever I changed back to a design that was used years ago, before being changed sometime in the 1980s to a geometry that wasn't correct because it caused the angle of pull on the cable to change dramatically during the course of its travel. I studied the geometry and put it back to the way it had been. Brilliant, huh?"

Prototype to Production

The full-fairing prototype Daytona made its debut at the Milan exposition in November 1989. It was a beautiful machine, with strong visual links to Wittner's latest racer provided by the aluminum "boomerang" sideplates and the general shape of the frame, tank, and fairing. Both carbureted and injected production versions were promised, but the prototype shown in Milan and first tested for magazine reviews was fitted with 40-millimeter Dell'Ortos because the street-going injection system was not yet ready. With favorable reviews, the effort to get the production machine ready redoubled, with delivery of the first machines promised for April 1990. Even so, because of many problems and a small design staff, the first production machines wouldn't be ready for more than two years.

Wittner continued: "I did a lot of race testing with Cees Doorakkers [a Dutchman and top privateer racer on the world championship circuit who rode the Daytona racer after Doug Brauneck was injured in a crash at Monza], but the racing was going away at that point because they really wanted me working to get the Daytona into production, and the bike was late. So I was put in charge of the Daytona project—still not speaking more than one and a half words of Italian, but somehow I managed.

"For years, De Tomaso's attention had been occupied almost exclusively in fixing the problems at Maserati. By the time I entered the picture he had solved many of those problems. He now had time to devote to Moto Guzzi. When I started

working there, it was Todero, myself, Giancarlo Lozza [a designer who has been at Moto Guzzi more than 50 years], and Marco Mauri [who was in charge of the experimental department], and we took care of not only the new models but also solving problems on the models that were already in production, so there wasn't really much of a possibility to move forward quickly. There just weren't the human resources to do it.

Cylinder-Head Problems

"[The Daytona] was delayed in production testing because that motorcycle had to perform at much-leaner air-fuel ratios and carry mufflers, so the cylinder head got so much hotter than it did in racing form, where I could use all the fuel I wanted to cool it off. The cylinder heads got so hot that normal cylinder-head alloys were inadequate. We began to search for solutions and finally found an alloy that would resist the temperatures, but we had to learn how to cast and heat treat it—and it's rather delicate. That's what we produce the cylinder heads from today, but it delayed the introduction of the Daytona by approximately a year.

"You have to realize that in the scheme of things, no one else was attempting to produce air-cooled motorcycle engines that have this much horsepower. Such engines present their own particular problems, and those problems are not easy to solve. The last road version of the Daytona has 108 horsepower at the crankshaft.

New Styling

"Santiago De Tomaso wanted to build a limited series of 200–300 Daytonas that were styled like the prototype, but unfortunately that didn't happen because of the delay caused by the need to find the right alloy for the cylinder heads. During that year, we had acquired a chief engineer named Paulo Brutti and a

The Corsa, a limited edition Sport for 1998. The package includes a carbon-fiber front fender, carbon-fiber mufflers (supplied in addition to the stock mufflers), black-anodized sideplates, black wheels and engine, chrome valve covers, and revised graphics. Two hundred are scheduled to be built. *Moto Guzzi* stylist named Adriano Galarsi, and these guys have good taste in motorcycles. They wanted to make the Daytona look a lot better than that first prototype did, and I think they were right. Without modifying the major mechanical aspects of the motorcycle, they changed its look and all its controls to make a motorcycle that I think is absolutely gorgeous.

"The last motorcycle we tested in our own wind tunnel was the Daytona, and I reinstrumented the wind tunnel at that point and found that the throat of the tunnel was really too small for modern motorcycles. It was constructed for full-fairing GP bikes of the 1950s, which had much smaller frontal areas. Even so, we made enormous improvements in the stability of the restyled Daytona, and in lowering its lift and total drag coefficient. [As it had been in the 1970s, wind-tunnel testing for the Daytona was done after hours because the power supply is inadequate to run both the factory and the wind tunnel. Moto Guzzi now conducts wind-tunnel testing at various Italian universities.]

The frame was redesigned to make it narrower and stiffer through the swingarm area on the fuel-injected Sport 1100 and Daytona RS. Other updates include a new sump with a filter that can be changed without removing the sump (at last!), an oil cooler with thermostatic valve mounted to the front of the sump, Dutch WP upside-down forks, Marchesini wheels (with cush drive), redesigned boomerang sideplates, and better brakes.

The Daytona RS is a retuned Daytona engine with the same chassis, suspension, and dynamic air intake of the injected Sport 1100. Changes to the engine include higher compression, Carillo rods, the camshafts from the C racing kit, and forged pistons.

Carbureted Daytona

"In 1990, we were planning a carbureted Daytona, but in the end, we only made the injected versions, for a lot of reasons. The American market really drove that decision because we wanted all the motorcycles we sent to the United States to be certified for California. The only good way to do that is with fuel injection. It makes it so much easier because you don't have evaporation from float bowls.

Daytona Exhaust and "Colostomy Bag" Collector

"There were two reasons for the header-pipe shape we ultimately used, which was much different than that of the prototype and the racer. Number one, we had to get the correct length between the heads and what we call the expansion chamber in order to get the powerband that we wanted. It could have been done in some other way, but frankly I liked the look of sharply bent-back pipes on sport bikes.

"The bends are different on the race-kit exhausts to get different tube lengths for different power characteristics. That was one of my projects. That came out of the work that I did for the race bikes. At a certain point, even race bikes had to be muffled. The AMA and the FIM imposed sound limits. I was scared to death worrying how I was going to get the horsepower through silencers. During that I learned a tremendous amount. I came up with the design for that collector in the center and mathematically figured out what I needed to do

there, and it was gratifying to learn that we could actually get a lot more horsepower with silencers than we ever got with open exhaust. That exhaust gave probably the biggest bump in horsepower that we got while developing that motorcycle.

"We made the Daytona exhaust of stainless steel because customers simply wanted an exhaust system that wouldn't rust. It was a very expensive motorcycle, and we decided it would get a stainless exhaust.

Two-Seat Daytonas

"The Daytona was designed as a single-seater, but dealers insisted on a two-seat version. We didn't really want to make that two-seater because the things that we had to house under the cowling just required a certain form. We didn't like the aesthetics of the rear end of the two-seater. We messed around with the style, but there was really nothing to be done until we redesigned the airbox and battery positions for the 1100 Sport."

Production Daytona

When the Daytona was released in extremely limited numbers beginning in spring 1992, it was the first truly, fundamentally new Guzzi since the V7 Sport of 1971. Even the press seemed to take notice, giving it good reviews for its smooth, powerful engine, light throttle, crisp response, fairly agile but stable steering, excellent suspension, improved shifting, lack of shaft-drive jacking, and swoopy modern styling. Reviewers almost universally (and justifiably) criticized the awkward and unstable sidestand and the poor finish on some examples. The price was also very high, $13,990 in the United States. Even so, advance orders for the machine would not be completely filled until the fall of 1993. The first Daytona to reach U.S. shores was flown in, along with Dr. John Wittner, for Moto America's open house on April 26, 1992.

The first series were all monopostos, fitted with an adjustable Koni shock in the rear, but the adjustments were difficult to reach and required removal of the seat cowling. Proper setup for pre-load is critical on the Daytona rear suspension to retain the proper squat characteristics, so two springs were available for the rear shock, a black one for riders weighing less than 187 pounds (85 kilograms), and a red one for heavier riders. Rear frame sections, battery, and other details are different on the monos and duos, such that the mono seat and tailpiece can be retrofitted to duo bikes, but not vice versa.

Forks are 41.7-millimeter Marzocchi M1Rs with three-position adjustments for compression and rebound damping. The front wheel is a cast 17-incher, and the rear is a cast 18-incher. The rear wheel lacks a cush drive. With its low clip-ons, high rearsets, and long reach from seat to tank, the riding position is a bit uncomfortable, except for those of simian build. Even so, it is not quite as extreme and cramped as, say, a Ducati 916.

All production Daytonas were fitted with Weber-Marelli fuel injection and electronic ignition. The system uses twin 50-millimeter throttle bodies and P7 electronics. It is an open-loop system that relies totally on "maps" stored on an EPROM in a box in the tail section. These maps adjust the ignition timing and injection based on inputs from throttle-position, rpm, and manifold vacuum sensors. It cannot self-compensate for changes to the intake or exhaust that change fuel-air mixture requirements, so any such changes require a new EPROM with appropriate maps to compensate. Fuel to the system is supplied by a pump. Triggers for the injection and ignition are attached to the flywheel, which is much lighter than on any previous Guzzi V-twin. Three performance kits were offered. Kit A includes a performance exhaust, foam air cleaners, and a revised EPROM. Kit B includes all of Kit A plus lightened engine internals. Kit C includes all of Kit B plus revised cams and a different fuel-pressure regulator. A very limited edition track-only version of the Daytona was also available. It lacked lights and was fitted with the C racing kit.

The transmission was substantially revised to improve shifting compared to the clunky gearboxes on the more pedestrian Guzzis. Gears in the Daytona transmission are straight-cut, with only three engagement dogs each (versus six), so gear-change action is quicker, at the cost of slightly more backlash.

Brakes are 300-millimeter Brembo stainless-steel floaters in front, squeezed by Brembo Gold Line four-piston calipers, and the rear is a solidly mounted 260-millimeter disc, with a two-piston Brembo caliper. Brakes are conventionally actuated, rather than of the standard Guzzi integrated design.

On Daytonas for the American, Australian, British, and Japanese markets, the headlight opening on the fairing is rectangular; for other markets, the opening is trapezoidal, wider at the top than at the bottom. In addition to the regular Daytona, a special Dr. John Replica was built for the British market in 1994, at the request of Keith Davies at Three Cross, the British importer of Moto Guzzis. These were monopostos with the B racing kit installed at the factory. They are painted black (with silver fork sliders) and have a "Dr. John" signature transfer on the tailpiece.

Daytonas were available in red, black, or silver. Most have fork legs painted the same color as the bodywork, but some red machines and black machines have silver sliders.

Changes

Part-way through the production run a guard was added to cover the exposed U-joint. Early Daytonas were recalled to add the guard. In November 1993, the transmission cush-drive spring was replaced by a stack of eight bent washers that do a better job of taking up the shock loads resulting from the lack of cush drive on the wheel. Starting partway through 1994, an updated version of the ignition/injection box, the P8, was phased into production. Also in 1994, an improved U-joint, with grease fittings, was phased in, as were 320-millimeter front brake rotors and five-position adjustable fork dampers like those on the Sport 1100. Some late Daytonas also have the Sport 1100-type exhaust. The Daytona was phased out in 1996, in favor of a restyled and updated version, the Daytona RS.

Daytona Racing

In 1996, the last variant of the original Daytona was offered, the Daytona Racing. It was street legal (in some countries) and was fitted with the C racing kit and "Dr. John Replica" transfers. Only 100 of this variant were made.

Sport 1100

Before the Daytona had even been released, the realists within the company knew that it would be a limited-production machine because of its price. Thoughts turned to making a Daytona for the masses—powered by a two-valve motor with carburetors so it could be lighter, cheaper, and more easily modified. A lot of people were talking about it in the R&D department. All they needed was an opportunity to bring the idea up to the boss and somebody willing to stick his neck out. The opportunity came at a meeting between De Tomaso, Wittner, Todero, and others, and Wittner was the one

The Centauro was styled by Luigi Marabese into the Italian ideal of the muscle-bike look. The styling is "love it or hate it." Plenty of Guzzi fans love it, and really love the combination of a Daytona motor (retuned for more torque), gearing, riding position, brakes, and suspension. For most people, this model is more comfortable than the Sport. The Centauro's pegs are lower and farther forward, and its flat bar is mounted on a short riser. Like the injected Sport, the Centauro was fitted with the new sump that allows changing the oil filter with the sump in place.

to give voice to the idea, suggesting that they put the two-valve motor in the Daytona chassis, but that they build a larger motor for the job. De Tomaso approved the idea for study, and work began, with the stipulation that the increased displacement could not come at the cost of redesigning the crankcase, according to Todero.

Todero and Wittner studied the task. The main constraint turned out to be the size of the hole in the crankcase for the cylinder spigot. Enlarging the hole had already been ruled out by De Tomaso, and 92 millimeters was as large a bore as they could safely manage under that constraint. With a 92-millimeter bore and the standard 78-millimeter stroke, that only got them from 949 cc to 992 cc, not enough to gain any meaningful marketing or power advantage compared to the standard engine. After all, the 949 was already sold as a 1,000. What would they call this, a *real* 1,000? The only option left was to increase the stroke, which would require a new crank. Todero and Wittner

settled on a stroke of 80 millimeters, for a displacement of 1,064 cc—a modest increase, but one that gave a useful increase in power and torque and got them close enough to 1,100 cc to call the new engine an 1100. De Tomaso approved their plan.

Then, the real work began. In the end, most of the major components of the engine were changed—cylinder heads, pistons, cylinders, crankshaft, connecting rods, camshaft, pushrods, and more, either to beef up the whole unit for the increased power and torque or to accommodate the electronic ignition that was an integral part of the design.

Camshafts for the new engine were a collaboration between Wittner and Chase Knight and David Bly of Crane Cams. Said Wittner, "Our design goals were to get a cam design that gave us the right performance and reduced mechanical noise from the top end. With a well-designed cam lobe, you accomplish both very easily. You get more power with more conservative valve timing when the valve can follow the accelerations of the cam lobe.

Crane hit the performance parameters we wanted with the first lobe they gave us."

Tachometer and ignition timer drives were left off the new cam because the Digiplex ignition was designed in from the start. The valves on the new heads were actually decreased in diameter 0.5 millimeter compared to those on the big-valve motor, to 46.5 millimeters intake and 39.5 millimeters exhaust. New, more progressive valve springs and steel collars complement the new valves and heads. New pistons with a low deck height and higher dome give a compression ratio of 9.5:1. (The original spec sheets list a compression ratio of 10.5:1, but the ratio was decreased to 9.5:1 late in development testing.) Connecting rods were strengthened by designing them so the rod bolts thread directly into bosses on the rod, without need for nuts. This also left clearance for bigger camshaft lobes.

Remember Lino Tonti's description of 16-inch wheels being the "mode of the moment"? Well, pressurized airboxes were the mode of the moment in the early 1990s. They're a great idea, in theory, but no one seems to have made such a system work well on a carbureted street bike. Nevertheless, Wittner gave it a try for the new Sport 1100. Despite countless hours of development work and the testing of many potential solutions, he fell prey to the same phenomenon that has stymied everyone else. As is his custom, he was remarkably frank on the subject:

"The carbureted bikes have a hole in the powerband because of pulses in the airbox. These pulses confuse the carburetor and cause a depression in the float chamber so that it doesn't deliver fuel when it ought to; it leans it out a little too much. And the confusion is made worse by the lean jetting needed to pass emissions tests. We tried all kinds of things to damp out the waves, and nothing was effective. We really tore our hair out over that, and were not happy about releasing the bike with that running fault, but sometimes you have to live with such limitations because the alternative is bankruptcy."

In defense of the effort, the pressurized box does add a few miles per hour to the top speed. Unfortunately, it does little except cause an annoying flat spot at more normal speeds. But then again, the whole idea behind the carbureted Sport was to allow the owner maximum latitude to tinker. And with a little tinkering, the flat spot goes away.

During development of the Sport, Mikuni flat-slide carbs were experimented with. Ultimately, 40-millimeter Dell'Orto PHMs were fitted because, according to Wittner, "The price of the motorcycle with the Mikunis would have been within about $250 of fuel injection." Also, Mikuni didn't have facilities in Europe to help with emissions testing.

Dozens of upgrades were made to the Sport chassis (compared to the Daytona chassis), including more curvaceous bodywork, lower footpegs, lighter 10-spring flywheel, 320-millimeter front discs (late Daytonas had this update), grease fittings on the U-joint and an access hole on the swingarm, sealed double-row swingarm bearings (replacing tapered roller bearings), and maintenance-free batteries (two

For 1998, the Centauro is offered in GT and Sport trim. Both Centuaros get redesigned seats, adjustable bars, and revised graphics. In addition, the Sport gets a handlebar-mounted fairing and a sump fairing. The GT gets a tiny luggage rack and an optional fairing and hard bags. *Moto Guzzi*

The different color combinations change the look of the Centauro by emphasizing or de-emphasizing the side panels. This one's either a real eye-catcher or an eye-sore, depending on individual taste. *Moto Guzzi*

per motorcycle). Sport 1100s for England, Japan, and the United States have a rectangular headlight. Those for other markets have a trapezoidal headlight.

Production

The Sport 1100 was introduced in the fall of 1993, with production slated to start shortly thereafter. Unfortunately, the Sport was late by almost a year, with bikes beginning to trickle down to dealers in the fall of 1994. The problem? According to Wittner: "Our development team was tiny; we simply couldn't accomplish what we wanted to do in the time we had to do it. The whole styling was changed after the introduction, there were minor changes made to the frame to facilitate production, and we changed the entire air-intake system, and that took a lot of development. There were only four of us, and we had nothing. At a regular company, you put about 50 on a project like that. To say we were strained would not be an exaggeration."

Initially, the Sport was available in black, red, or silver, with fork sliders painted to match. A short while later, metallic midnight blue was added. And shortly after that, the fork sliders for all color schemes were painted silver.

Stylistically and functionally, the Sport 1100 was a success. And with a U.S. retail price under $10,000, the Sport sold well in its first year. It was

back for 1996 with just a few changes. Unfortunately, sales died off because the new injected Sport (the Sport 1100i) was announced, so many buyers chose to wait for the upgraded model. Unfortunately, the 1100i didn't reach the market until fall, so many potential 1996 sales were lost.

Sport 1100i

In late 1996, a new Sport was released, the Sport 1100i, with fuel injection and a host of other significant upgrades that made it a better motorcycle, if not a better value. It was fitted with the latest version of the Weber-Marelli fuel-injection system (the 16M), using 45-millimeter throttle bodies. With fuel injection, the pulses in the dynamic airbox are no longer of concern, so the midrange flat spot largely disappeared. Even with fuel injection, however, it is a real challenge to comply with the latest emissions regulations while still providing smooth throttle response. Consequently, changes to the EPROM maps and the exhaust system are sometimes necessary to get a truly smooth response. The other major engine change was to a new sump spacer and pan that includes an oil cooler and, at long last, an access port to allow changing the oil filter without first removing the sump.

Chassis, suspension, and wheel upgrades were also significant. The frame was made narrower and stiffer in the swingarm-pivot area, and restyled alloy sideplates replaced the old "boomerangs." Oval-section tubing replaced square tubing on the swingarm. Top-of-the-line Dutch WP forks and Marchesini wheels were fitted front and rear. The rear even included a cush drive, an important feature that had been missing on earlier spine-frames. The first injected Sports had the Daytona-type straight-cut transmission gears. Later models got new helical gears. Some later machines were fitted with Brembo wheels.

Guzzi even got around to at least partially fixing two gripe-worthy features of earlier Sports. First, the "Sport 1100" graphics (easily misread as "Spot 1100") were replaced by impossible-to-misread "1100 Sport" decals. Second, the sidestand was revised to move it rearward just a bit. It's still difficult to deploy from the saddle and unsteady, but slightly improved on both counts. The 1100i was available in red, black, and yellow.

Compared to the earlier Sport, weight was up over 30 pounds. And all those pricey additions—injection, fork, wheels—drove up the price enough

that sales fell way below projections, at least in the United States. In the fall of 1997, the importer dropped the price to dealers to clear the warehouse, and Sport prices fell to about the same as for the new Ducati replicas from Japan. The Sports quickly sold out. The Sport 1100i was not sold as a 1998 U.S. model.

For 1998, the Sport 1100i Corsa Limited Edition was introduced. Special features of the Corsa include Carillo rods, carbon-fiber mufflers (supplied in addition to the stainless-steel mufflers), black engine (with bright valve covers), black-anodized sideplates, black wheels, revised graphics, cast-iron floating front discs, and others. The 200 Corsas built were painted red or yellow. As of this writing Moto Guzzi planned to discontinue the Sport 1100 in 1998.

Daytona RS

Also introduced fall of 1996 was an updated version of the Daytona, the RS, a model created by fitting an updated Daytona engine to the same basic chassis used on the Sport 1100i. Updates to the

The Quota was introduced at the Milan exposition in 1989. For those with long legs, it makes a comfortable all-around bike, like the BMW GS series. A 1991 1000 Quota is shown here. *Moto Guzzi*

engine include the new sump spacer and pan with integral oil cooler, forged pistons supplying higher compression (10.5:1 versus 10:1), camshafts from the racing C kit (except on variants for the United States, Switzerland, and Singapore, which used the original Daytona cams), Carillo connecting rods, and the lighter flywheel of the Sport 1100i. The RS got a lower 160/60-17 rear tire than the Sport 1100i's 160/70-17 and an appropriately different speedo drive gear. The RS also gets its own tach, redlining at 9,000 rpm. Basically, it is a more powerful rendition of the 1100 Sport or a better handling Daytona.

V10 Centauro

Another "mode of the moment" seems to be bare muscle bikes. Following the herd, Guzzi ripped the clothes off the Daytona RS, retuned the four-valve motor for more torque, and hired noted Italian industrial designer Luigi Marabese to design for it abbreviated new clothes. The result is the Centauro, which I think shows a new level of self-confidence at Moto Guzzi because its styling purposely polarizes opinion—you either see it as a bold, make-you-drool machine or a reprise of the "mutant Tupperware designer" bikes—and everything other than the former is a lost sale. The engine has a rare combination of torque and top-end power, with perfect gearing to make use of both; the suspension and brakes are superb; and the control locations suit many riders. The Centauro was introduced in November 1995, but the first series of Centauros (sold in selected markets) wasn't ready until November 1996. These bikes differed in many small details from the regular production Centauros that soon followed. The first Centauros reached most markets in early 1997.

The Centauro engine is basically the Daytona RS engine with camshafts from the original Daytona, a non-pressurized airbox, and a coat of anthracite paint. Rare in the case of a Guzzi, magazine reviewers even loved the engine (although none of them could resist dredging up the Myth of the Mule). In a "Hell-Raisers" shoot-out against a Buell, a Ducati, and a Triumph in the November 1997 *Cycle World*, the Centauro was found to be the quickest, fastest, and most powerful of the four. The editors also declared it "Guzzi's best effort ever."

Unfortunately, it didn't sell well, at least in the United States. Its biggest handicap is its $13,000 retail price, making it far and away the most expensive bike of its type. For 1997, Centauros were available in yellow and black, red and gray, and all gray.

For 1998, little was changed, except that the sidestand was updated and the Centauro was offered in two additional variations, the GT and the Sport. The GT is a bizarre attempt to give the Centauro the aura of a light-duty touring machine by fitting the briefest of windshields, adjustable handlebars, a restyled seat, and a stylized suggestion of a luggage rack at the back. Optional hard bags are also offered. The Centauro Sport is the basic Centauro with a bit more Tupperware, in the form of a chin fairing and a small headlight fairing, along with adjustable handlebars, a restyled seat, and new graphics. Colors for the Sport are red or British racing green.

V11 Sport

A new-generation basic sporter is scheduled to be released in fall 1998, the V11 Sport, which is being billed as a V7 Sport for the twenty-first century. Moto Guzzi even painted one of the prototypes like a *Telaio Rosso* V7 Sport, perhaps a mistake. While a minority like the combination of lime green with a red frame, the majority find it just too gaudy. Even so, the buzz surrounding this model surpasses that of any Moto Guzzi in recent memory. Even non-*Guzzisti* comment on what an intriguing package it appears to be. If it is priced right, and proper accessories are offered (including a stylish and effective add-on fairing), this could be the breakthrough model the company has needed for many years.

Although the prototypes of the V11 Sport are fitted with a five-speed transmission, production V11 Sports are scheduled to ship with an all-new six-speed transmission that is being tested on the Ippogrifo prototypes. The torquey Moto Guzzi engine probably needs a sixth gear about as much as it needs a third cylinder. Even so, the new transmission brings with it benefits far more important than the extra gear. Overall, it is shorter by 1.97 inches (50 millimeters) and the output shaft is lowered by 0.79 inch (20 millimeters), which will allow use of a longer driveshaft (without increasing wheelbase) and a reduced angle on the U-joints for longer life. It also allows greater latitude in positioning the engine in the frame. Wittner has hinted that the angle of the engine may be reduced from its present two degrees to a lesser angle to help bring the polar moment of inertia of the engine and motorcycle more nearly in line. This new transmission bolts up to the standard Guzzi engine, so it will likely be retrofitted to revised versions of the other models in the near future.

The engine is the basic Guzzi 1,064-cc V-twin from the Sport 1100i, with lightened internal components and the oil cooler moved from the front of the sump to a new location across the frame below the steering head.

Quota 1000

At the Milan exposition in the fall of 1989, Moto Guzzi introduced a new model to compete with the big-bore off-road bikes from BMW, Cagiva, Honda, and Yamaha. Though officially launched at the end of 1989, the production machines weren't widely available until almost two years later.

Dr. John's dirt bike, the Quota ES, is scheduled for release in the summer of 1998. This latest version of the Quota features a seat height lowered by almost 3 inches, updated styling, and a version of the 1,064-cc EV motor with a central throttle body and long intake manifolds to produce a very wide powerband. *Moto Guzzi*

According to Wittner, the Quota was designed at the behest of Paulo Donghi, managing director of Moto Guzzi at the time, who was a great fan of off-road competition during his days at Benelli and who even had Moto Guzzi build 125-cc off-road racers in a house near the factory for a youth competition series.

Guzzi engineers designed for the Quota a twin-spar frame of square-section tubing, with a long-travel monoshock (with a linkage) rear suspension. In that frame they stuck the medium-valve motor and five-speed transmission. The engine is unique in that both cylinders are fed by a central Weber-Marelli throttle body with a long, smooth manifold to each cylinder, and the ignition is controlled by a digital engine management system. The exhaust system is stainless steel, consisting of twin header pipes, a large crossover under the transmission, and a large muffler on the right side. With these systems, the Quota's powerband is optimized for low-rpm torque, precisely the kind of power it needs.

The rear shock is a Marzocchi unit, as is the leading-axle front fork. Separate brake systems are used front and rear (non-integrated). Twin 280-millimeter front discs are squeezed by Grimeca four-piston calipers. Rear braking is supplied by a single 260-millimeter iron disc and a Brembo caliper. Tube-type alloy rims are fitted front and rear, shod with a 90/90-21 Pirelli universal in front

and a 130/80-17 in the rear. The suspension is softly sprung, giving a very plush ride on the road, but is reportedly too soft for any but the slowest off-road riding. With such soft springs in the rear, the rear end jacks up and down enthusiastically when you get on and off the power, so much so that *Fast Bikes* magazine (November 1991), observed wryly that "the Quota must be the only motorcycle in the world where you drop the clutch and the back end comes up first."

From the frame-mounted fairing with twin headlights, to the 5.3-gallon (20-liter) fuel tank with flush-mounted filler, to the tapered tailpiece with its small luggage rack, the bodywork is styled as an integrated whole, painted in red or a dark blue-black. In comparing the Quota to the BMW GS series, *Fast Bikes* magazine (November 1991) said, "some [Germans] prefer it to the indigenous Boxer not just because ultimately, the design is more versatile, but because the Guzzi oozes the one ingredient the perfect race just seems incapable of producing—style."

The Quota remained available intermittently through 1997, and was sold in most world markets, but was not imported into the United States.

Quota 1100 ES: Dr. John's Dirt Bike

Guided by project manager Dr. John Wittner, a substantially revised Quota is scheduled to be introduced midyear 1998, the Quota 1100 ES (Enduro Stradale). The major upgrade is use of the 1,064-cc EV motor, with an updated central-body injector system that is said to make the already torquey 1100 engine even more so. Guzzi claims the torque peaks at 3,800 rpm, and that it retains 90 percent of that peak from 2,800 rpm to 5,800 rpm. The secret to all this torque is the central throttle body and long intake manifolds, along with a balance pipe between the two header pipes, near the front of the engine (photos of the prototype do not show this pipe, however). According to Wittner, "The 1100 motor with that intake and exhaust has 25 percent more torque at 2,500 rpm than a California 1100, and it has the same peak horsepower."

Wittner's design team didn't neglect the Quota chassis, either. One of the major complaints about the Quota had long been its seat height, which was about 35 inches (885 millimeters). Chassis revisions allowed them to lower it by about 2.8 inches (70 millimeters), still rather tall, but about the same as for other bikes in this class. Other notable upgrades include stainless-steel discs (twin 296-millimeter front and 260-millimeter rear), Brembo Gold Line calipers at the front, improved Marzocchi fork and shock, and improved electrics. All these changes should make a good bike even better. Said Wittner: "It is a fabulous motorcycle—the most comfortable motorcycle we've ever built, and it has the nicest powerband. We're put-

The V11 Sport is scheduled for release in fall 1998 in single- and dual-seat versions. We'll see if the *Telaio Rosso* replica paint scheme shown on this prototype makes it into production. The technical highlight of the Sport is a six-speed transmission that is being developed on the 750-cc Ippogrifo. *Moto Guzzi*

ting long, tall ratios on the thing because it is really intended as a touring bike." Fortunately, Moto America plans to bring some Stateside.

The Future

Moto Guzzi has shown more vitality in the last five years than it did in the previous 20. In place now are new management and important refinements to the machines (such as much lighter flywheels, electronic ignition, and fuel injection). To come, according to reports, are new production facilities in Monza and next-generation air-cooled and water-cooled engines and a variety of new bikes. The water-cooled engine will reportedly be a 75-degree V-twin with true overhead cams and chain-drive that will first power an all-out sport twin, and then other models. The air-cooled

engine will likely be larger in displacement than the current 1100 and will be much shorter in length to accommodate a more modern chassis for a variety of new models, possibly including an "Eldorado in modern key" (Dr. John Wittner's description). Also in the works are a big thumper and a line of scooters.

Even jaded editors of motorcycle magazines are starting to cautiously mention the word "turnaround" when talking about Moto Guzzi. Will Guzzi's turnaround be as dramatic as Harley-Davidson's? Not likely, but it could equal Ducati's, and that level of success would be a remarkable enough achievement and a fitting start for Moto Guzzi in the new millennium.

INDEX